CHRISTIANITY AND CRAFT FREEMASONRY
A PASTORAL GUIDE FOR CHRISTIAN MINISTERS

GERARD G. MOATE

The Latimer Trust

The Latimer Trust (formerly Latimer House, Oxford) is a conservative
Evangelical research organisation within the Church of England, whose
main aim is to promote the history and theology of Anglicanism as
understood by those in the Reformed tradition. Interested readers are
welcome to consult its website for further details of its many activities.

The Latimer Trust
London N14 4PS UK
Registered Charity: 1084337
Company Number: 4104465
Web: www.latimertrust.org
E-mail: administrator@latimertrust.org

CONTENTS

Foreword to the Revised Edition

Why revise a study more than thirty years after it was first published? More particularly, why do this when it is a study about a Christian response to Freemasonry – a subject that seems esoteric at best and is, to judge by the silence, not currently an issue?

First, I was asked to do so by the publishers some years ago but that invitation came at a difficult time for me to give the task the sustained attention it required. Second, the format of the first edition, limited by the budget and technology of the time, was published in a typewriter font. Third, this study was originally published before the internet was generally available and at a time when getting access to books on this subject was very much harder. Now, although there is much to be found on the internet, sifting it and testing the veracity of this information is not easy. In the process of making corrections and deletions and of adding a few paragraphs to span the years between then and now, it has also been thought helpful to point the reader to some reliable online resources.

Not everything has been retained; some pages in the first edition, such as a briefing paper for the debate in General Synod in 1987, now seem redundant. The few illustrations have been omitted because they are easily found and better examined online. In their place are appendices to help with Masonic abbreviations, esoteric rituals and vocabulary. The bibliography has been revised and expanded to include British Library shelf marks so that others may consider for themselves what has been examined here.

Lastly, although this study was originally written at a time when Freemasonry was in the public eye in Britain, it had a purpose which does not cease to be useful simply because it is not topical. Above all it was written for Christian ministers and church leaders, so that they might be equipped to respond wisely and well to Freemasons they meet in their churches, on their councils or boards, or as pillars of their communities. If this revised study continues to serve that purpose then it will honour our loving God who in every age 'will bring to light what is hidden in darkness and will expose the motives of the heart' (1 Cor 4:5).

Windrush
January 2021

PREFACE (FROM THE PREFACE TO THE FIRST EDITION)

Mention the word 'Freemason' to a man and he is quite likely to tug at one of his trouser legs, in a mocking reference to their reputation for strange rituals, or at the very least make some joke at their expense. Unless, of course, he is one himself.

About half a million men in England and Wales are Freemasons.[1] They tend to be men in the higher socio-economic groups and proudly include royalty among their membership. They have a reputation for generosity, at least towards one another, and the more commonly known fact about them is that they enjoy secrecy.

This present consideration of the tenets and practices of Freemasonry can make no claim to be entirely objective, but it is hoped that it will be found to be accurate in detail and thorough in discussion. It is primarily intended to be of use to Christian ministers, who may be required to give their opinions, or provide pastoral guidance about Freemasonry – about which they may know little. At the same time, it may provoke discussion among other Christians as to whether a dual allegiance, to Christianity and Freemasonry, is a genuine option available to a thoughtful Christian man.

Hampstead
July 1987

---

[1] In 2020, United Grand Lodge of England (UGLE) now claims only 'over 200,000'.
https://www.ugle.org.uk/10-faq/43-how-many-freemasons-are-there (accessed 30 April 2020).

1. The Greatest Secret of Freemasonry

A secret society?

What can be known about a secret society? If it is truly secret, the answer is next to nothing. Yet this study is not the paradox which it may at first seem to be. No worldwide organisation which claims to have six million members can expect to remain completely secret.[2] In Britain, more than any other country, Freemasons have at times endeavoured to maintain a silence about their affairs. A result is the commonly held belief that authentic information about Freemasonry is impossible to obtain. It is important to explain why this is not true.

From the beginning of Craft Freemasonry in England during the seventeenth century there have been disclosures.[3] In 1730, Samuel Prichard, an ex-Mason, published *Masonry Dissected*, which was the first widely circulated and largely authentic exposure.[4] Since then there have been several other ex-Masons who have gone into print, with varying degrees of prejudice, who have provided a curious public with information and upon which fantasy has been able to flourish.

Fascinated or alarmed by such disclosures, non-Masons have given detailed, if sporadic, attention to Freemasonry. This has mostly been from a religious standpoint, such as that by Walton Hannah, in the early 1950s.[5] The thoroughness and detail of Hannah's research is unsurpassed by any other non-Mason.

---

[2] https://www.ugle.org.uk/10-faq/43-how-many-freemasons-are-there (accessed 7 May 2020).

[3] 'Craft' is a term used for mainstream Freemasonry in England and Wales, under the direction of the United Grand Lodge of England (UGLE) in London.

[4] Samuel Prichard, *Masonry Dissected: being a universal and genuine description of all its branches from the original to this present time* (London: J. Wilford, 1730). An irony is that Masonic writers use Prichard's work and another exposure by Richard Carlile, *The Manual of Freemasonry* (1825), to substantiate matters of detail where historic Masonic records are missing.

[5] Walton Hannah (1912–66); see Bibliography.

In 1965, James Dewar produced a TV documentary for BBC Television, called 'The Open Secret', in which, for the first time, parts of some Masonic rituals were shown in public, acted by non-Masons.[6]

Such was the scorn of Freemasonry it provoked that, unsurprisingly, Masons reacted by considering virtually all their affairs worthy of 'privacy'. Honest enquiries, whether prompted by religious motives or not, were discouraged by senior Masons. James Stubbs, a former Grand Secretary of the United Grand Lodge of England (UGLE), responded to an enquiry by a chaplain, Robert Foxcroft, by saying 'You will prostitute anything you are told. Only a fool would talk to you.'[7] A 'society with secrets' (as the Craft prefers to be thought) had become, in effect, a secret society.

Unfortunately for the Craft it was too late. Many thousands of books have been written about Freemasonry and find their way onto the lists of second-hand booksellers.[8] Masonic rituals, catechisms and commentaries are widely available, often after having been discarded by the widows of Masons. These are printed in a manner supposedly only intelligible to Masons (with certain words indicated by their initial letter only) but the truth is that they are considerably easier to understand than many works of reference that affect no such secrecy.

Finally, there are practising Masons. Although in theory they are bound by oaths of secrecy, in practice it would seem that many are willing to talk about most aspects of Freemasonry, with the exception of the signs, hand-grips and passwords by which they recognise one another – and these may be learnt from other sources.[9] However, an important point to realise is that the average Mason is no more aware of what his brotherhood is, or what it does, than the average Church of England churchgoer is of the

---

[6] Research for that documentary was published: James Dewar, *The Unlocked Secret* (revised ed. 1990).

[7] Quoted in *The Listener*, 24 March 1980, 524.

[8] Back in 1964, the report of the *Commission of Inquiry into Secret Organisations*, Republic of South Africa, estimated more than 50,000 books and pamphlets (publ. 12 December 1964, RP20/1965).

[9] 'Freemasons are under no obligation to conceal their membership of the Craft and, in response to inquiries for respectable reasons, will gladly acknowledge it', *Freemasonry and Christianity*, being Grand Lodge's evidence to the Church of England Working Group (1987), Annex C2, 16.

Established Church. Indeed, because of historic pressure to maintain secrecy, even within the organisation, a Mason may know very much less.

The point of view of any member will therefore depend upon his breadth of experience, especially of places other than his local gathering. In Freemasonry, such experience is severely limited by the amount of money and time a member is prepared to give. The result is a surprising amount of ignorance among those whom one would expect to be well-informed.

Are there 'Inner Secrets'?

Nearly a century ago a Masonic writer admitted that the so-called 'inner secrets' of the Craft 'have been betrayed times out of number'.[10] What he, and many other disillusioned Masons, contend is that the real secret of Freemasonry is not a secret at all but rather a mystery, being the verbally incommunicable experience of a practising Mason. This mystery supposedly has its roots in the fellowship found only within the brotherhood of Freemasonry, which in its ideal form is an unalloyed trust of one another and is developed using the moral symbolism and allegory, as found within Masonic rituals, and applied to everyday life.

That there is a peculiarly esoteric experience to be found within Freemasonry cannot be doubted. With the great emphasis that is laid upon secret rituals and recognition, it would be surprising if there were not. However, there is quite a difference between specific secrets and an 'air of mystery'. Whereas the former is either known or they are not, the latter is more elusive – and yet may reasonably be understood through comparison with similar, more accessible, experiences. What passes for secrecy then, is really a preferred privacy, being a combination of bluff, ignorance and an assumption that the non-Mason is not sufficiently interested to investigate. The greatest secret that Freemasonry possesses, one which has been surprisingly well-kept, even from Masons, is that *there is no such thing as a specific Masonic secret.*

---

[10] A. E. Waite, *New Encyclopaedia of Freemasonry*, 1925, vol. II, 208.

2. WHAT IS FREEMASONRY?

An answer to this question would seem an obvious place to begin. It soon becomes clear that there is not a simple answer or convenient summary that would do justice even to the divergent interpretations provided by Freemasons themselves.[11]

One might as well try to answer the question, 'What is Anglicanism?', for the scope of reply may be similarly broad. Indeed, the problem of defining Anglicanism is usefully analogous, for it will give the reader some idea of the different answers that would be given to the question by, for example, official Masonic documents, office holders within the brotherhood, respected Masonic commentators, or any one of the general membership.

We will consider answers provided by all these sources, as well as non-Masonic writers, in looking at the origins, constitutions and rituals of Freemasonry, after which we may reasonably expect to at least have a balanced answer to the question.

Origins

The year 1717 is an important date in the history of Freemasonry in England. In that year, the first Grand Lodge of England had its birth. It has been observed that all Freemasonry in existence today can be traced, though one channel or another, to that first Grand Lodge in England.[12]

Much Masonic energy has been spent in establishing a more esoteric origin. Popular is a connection with medieval stonemasons, the builders of the great cathedrals and castles of Europe. It is known that they guarded professional secrets by the formation of guilds, which restricted their membership and provided a suitable forum for the advancement of their craft. In England, the stonemasons met in 'Lodges' and had secret passwords and methods of recognition. According to some Masonic histories it is from these so-called 'operative' stonemasons that

---

[11] In answer to the question 'What is Freemasonry?' the newly initiated Freemason is provided with a brief reply, which will be discussed below, but it is deliberately enigmatic and does not gainsay the point made here.

[12] Fred L. Pick and Gilfred N. Knight, *The Pocket History of Freemasonry* (London: Muller, 7th ed. 1983), 68, there quoting a Dr W. J. Chetwode Crawley.

'speculative' Freemasonry (i.e. 'non-operative') developed.[13] It is true that modern Craft Freemasonry leans heavily on symbolism drawn from the trade and tools of stonemasons (to which has since been added a code of morality), although a genuine connection between the two has not been established. On the contrary, other Masonic historians will admit:

> It can be very plausibly argued that a great deal of the symbolism which we find in the Craft today is actually a comparatively modern feature and that some was not introduced until after the beginning of the eighteenth century.[14]

Other influences claimed for Freemasonry include: the Knights Templar, Jewish Kabbalists, Egyptian mystery cults, Rosicrucianism and astrology. A Mason is free to believe that any or none of these are the origin of Freemasonry, although most Masons would probably agree with the following:

> Not only has no convincing evidence yet been brought forward to prove linear descent of our Craft from any organisation which is known to have, or even suspected of having, taught any similar system of morality, but also, from what we know of the Craft in the few centuries prior to the formation of the first Grand Lodge in 1717, it is excessively unlikely that there was any such parentage.[15]

The background to the events of St John the Baptist's Day, 24 June 1717, are contained in a few manuscripts of constitutions and minutes, the earliest dating from 1723. Earlier documents, often claimed to be relevant,

---

[13] Those, such as Craft Freemasons, who do not work with stone but who use the tools and skills of actual (operative) stonemasons in a philosophical or symbolic way as metaphors for living a good life. For an account of the transition: H. L. Haywood, 'How operative Masonry changed to speculative Masonry: the period of transition', *The Builder* (February 1924, X, 2);
http://www.freemasons-freemasonry.com/operative_speculative_masons.html (accessed 1 May 2020).
[14] Pick and Knight, *Pocket History*, 13.
[15] Pick and Knight, *Pocket History*, 13.

probably refer to 'operative' stonemasonry. Drawing heavily on a legendary history of the stonemason's craft, together with their rules, customs and traditions, several men were disposed to develop a speculative society and began to hold regular meetings in taverns.[16]

Their motives were probably as varied as their membership. There had been a growth of freedom of spirit in social, political, commercial and religious life in England. There was also a continuous decline of operative stonemasons throughout the seventeenth century as the period of building great cathedrals came to an end. Adopting that sub-culture, a new breed of men, fired by the Enlightenment, found a safe outlet for their increasing desire for freedom of speech. The appeal of a brotherhood, the comfort of charity within a restricted membership and, importantly, the regular use of secrecy, contributed to the early success of Craft Freemasonry.

In London, four Lodges (as Masonic groups are called), with a total membership of fewer than a hundred, took the step of organising a Grand Lodge and electing their first Grand Master. Within a few years from that first meeting, Freemasons had re-organised the ancient initiation ceremonies of the stonemasons, collected and collated their manuscripts and produced a set of constitutions. Various editions of this work provide a guide to the development of Freemasonry during the next three centuries.

Constitutions

Anthony Sayer, first Grand Master, was succeeded after a year by George Payne, who compiled a set of general *Regulations* in 1720. These concerned such matters as the authority of the Grand Master, the regularity and constitution of meetings, the admitting of new members and the need to preserve 'the old Landmarks'.[17] In 1723, James Anderson, 'a pedantic, pushing Presbyterian London minister' published a digested and revised version of several stonemasons' 'Old Charges' together with

---

[16] cf. William J. Hughan, *Masonic Sketches and Reprints*, part 3, 'The Old Charges of British Freemasons' (London: G. Kenning, 1871–79).

[17] 'Whatever is found necessary to maintain the identity and secure the perpetuity of Freemasonry has the property of a Landmark.' George Draffen, *The Making of a Mason* (London: A. Lewis, 1978), 18.

Payne's *Regulations*.[18] His book, *The Constitutions of the Freemasons*, presents an accurate view of the development and tenets of Freemasonry at that time.[19]

There were a few changes made to the legends of origin, but these were by no means the most significant changes. Whereas the 'Old Charges' had urged Masons to 'love God and his Holy Church', the First Charge of Anderson's *Constitutions* did not require of Freemasons any distinctively Christian belief:

> 'tis now thought more expedient only to oblige them
> to that Religion in which all men agree, leaving their
> particular opinions to themselves.[20]

Masonic writers disagree about the reason for the change. Some say it implied a change from Christianity to deism, in keeping with Enlightenment thinking. Others claim that it was a concession to Dissenters, of whom Anderson was one, or perhaps to practising Jews who were established members of the Lodges.[21]

Anderson also introduced phrases from Scottish 'operative' stonemasonry, such as 'Entered Apprentice', 'Fellowcraft', and 'Cowan' which have been retained.[22] By 1730, there were three distinct 'degrees' of Freemasonry, each having their own rituals based on fictional legends of the building of King Solomon's Temple. These remain the basis of all Masonic initiation and membership to this day.

---

[18] Alfred Robbins, *English-Speaking Freemasonry* (London: Ernest Benn, 1930), 35.

[19] The text of Payne's *Regulations* and Anderson's *Constitutions* is reproduced in Margaret Jacob, *The Radical Enlightenment: Pantheists, Freemasons and Republicans* (London: Allen & Unwin, 1981), 279–87.

[20] James Anderson, *The Constitutions of the Freemasons*, 1723, First Charge.

[21] Pick and Knight, *Pocket History*, 77. From earliest times some Masons were Jewish: for example, Benjamin Deluze and Simon Ansell (1723), Israel Segalas and Nicholas Abrahams (1725) and, by the 1730s, Solomon Mendez, Isaac Barrett and Moses Mendez are mentioned as being Grand Stewards responsible for organising Masonic festivals. Cf. Prof. Aubrey Newman, 'Jews in English Freemasonry', a lecture given to Israel Branch of the Jewish Historical Society of England in Jerusalem, 14 April 2015.

[22] See the Glossary.

By 1721, Freemasons had their first noble Grand Master in John Montagu.[23] Such was the success of this appointment in attracting membership from among the upper classes that Anderson enshrined in his *Constitutions*: 'No Brother can be a ... Grand Master unless he be nobly born, or a Gentleman of best fashion'.[24] Following Anderson's death in 1739, Freemasonry entered a period of decline. Attendance at Lodges and payment of dues became so lax that in 1743 Horace Walpole remarked:

> The Freemasons are in ... low repute now in England.
> I believe nothing but persecution could bring them
> into vogue again.[25]

Paradoxically it was not a persecution but a schism which rejuvenated Freemasonry. Opposition to the opening of the Craft to non-Christians, changes in the modes of recognition and a neglect of Masonic festivals led to the formation of a rival Grand Lodge in 1751. The 'Antients' [*sic*], as they were called, soon appointed their own noble Grand Master and re-introduced much that had been allowed to go by default.

Throughout the late-eighteenth century these two branches of the English Craft rivalled each other. The 'Moderns' (as the Antients called them) scored a significant victory when the Duke of Cumberland, brother of George III, was elected as Grand Master. This began a Masonic connection with royalty which has been maintained ever since.[26] Eventually it was realised that rivalry was in the interest of neither branch. In 1813, when royal brothers were Grand Masters of the two branches, Freemasonry came together as one organisation. The United Grand Lodge remains the governing body of Craft Freemasonry to this day.

The *Constitutions* were again revised in 1815. The so-called 'History of Freemasonry', which had long before been discredited, was omitted. A significant change was also made to the First Charge, 'Concerning God and Religion':

---

[23] John Montagu, 2nd Duke of Montagu (1690–1749).
[24] *Constitutions*, 1723, Fourth Charge.
[25] Cited by Pick and Knight, *Pocket History*, 87.
[26] Prince Edward, Duke of Kent (b. 1935), has been the Grand Master since 1967.

> Let a man's religion or mode of worship be what it
> may, he is not excluded from the order, provided he
> believe in the glorious Architect of heaven and earth,
> and practise the sacred duties of morality.[27]

In the name of 'fraternal love', the last specifically Christian content was removed from the *Constitutions*. This was a move towards deism, though it cannot therefore be concluded that this was intended to be anti-Christian but rather, to use a contemporary term, inclusive.

Today, every Freemason, after his initiation into the First Degree is given a copy of the *Constitutions*. In addition to Payne's *Regulations* and the 1815 revision of Anderson's *Constitutions*, it contains over 300 pages of organisational minutiae, in which will be found, as Rule 159, that 'his acceptance thereof shall be deemed a declaration of his submission to its contents'.[28] For the most part, these are typical of the rules governing any large voluntary organisation, though perhaps with a greater emphasis on regalia and the grandiose titles of its office holders. Of interest are the rules governing the initiation of a candidate and the organisation of a Lodge, which will now be considered.

Preparation for initiation

An examination of the motives for wanting to be a Freemason will be considered in chapter six. For now, it will be assumed that the candidate could honestly answer 'yes' to the following:

> Do you seriously declare on your honour that,
> unbiased by the improper solicitation of friends
> against your own inclination, and uninfluenced by
> mercenary or other unworthy motive, you freely and

---

[27] After more than thirty revisions of the *Constitutions* this is the wording that has endured.

[28] *Constitutions of the Antient Fraternity of Free and Accepted Masons* (London: UGLE, 1984), Rule 159.
This and other *Constitutions* rules cited here may have been re-numbered in more recent editions.

> voluntarily offer yourself a candidate for the mysteries and privileges of Freemasonry? [29]

How a candidate is prepared for initiation will depend upon several things:

- the Rules set out in the *Constitutions*
- the requirements found within the chosen form of Craft ritual
- to a lesser extent, local Lodge custom

A candidate must have been duly proposed by two paid-up Masons and complete an application form which will enable the Lodge to make a thorough examination of him. He will have been interviewed at a venue other than that of the regular Lodge, and asked various questions, where a wrong answer (such as 'no' to the question 'do you believe in God?') would mean immediate disqualification. He will have survived a secret balloting by the Lodge members (where, in some, even one vote against will bar candidacy) and only then receive an invitation to present himself for initiation.

Therefore, it is usually with some apprehension that a candidate will approach this event. It is, it seems, intended that he should feel that way, for little is done (except perhaps by his proposers) to put him at ease. The usual kind of reply to enquiries about what will happen at the initiation is 'don't worry, we've all been through it' – which only serves to increase his disquiet.

Two further stages remain before his initiation can begin. According to Rule 162, he must sign the following Declaration:

> I, (Full Name), being a free man, and of the age of twenty-one years, do declare that, unbiased by the improper solicitation of friends and uninfluenced by mercenary or other unworthy motive, I do freely and voluntarily offer myself a candidate for the mysteries of Masonry; that I am prompted by favourable impression conceived of the institution, and a desire of knowledge; and that I will cheerfully conform to all

---

[29] The first of three questions concerning his motives that a candidate is asked during his initiation into the First Degree.

the antient usages and the established customs of the Order.[30]

By the current Constitutions he must be an adult male and 'desiring knowledge'; furthermore, any 'petitioner must be a man, in the full sense of the word, not a woman, or a child, or a eunuch.' [31] Although women were permitted to become Masons elsewhere in Europe (for example, within the 'Grand Orient' Masonic jurisdiction), in England and Wales, and other places such as Scotland and the USA that eventually accepted these Constitutions, that possibility was excluded. In England, in the twentieth century, two exclusively female Masonic jurisdictions were established (see Appendix II). In some places, albeit on separate occasions, they share the use of 'regular' Craft Lodge premises.

In that Declaration he must also be prepared to 'cheerfully conform to all the antient usages and the established customs of the Order' before he can officially know what they are – since, by their nature, they are numbered among the 'mysteries' of Masonry which he has yet to experience.

Finally, he must be ritually prepared by the Tyler (who is required to keep non-Masons out of the Lodge) to go forward into the Temple (as the ceremonial room is called) where the anxious candidate is blindfolded and a noose of silk (called a 'cable-tow') is placed around his neck. Divested of his jacket, his shirt is partially removed to reveal his left breast and the right sleeve is rolled above his elbow. His left trouser leg is rolled up above his knee and his right shoe is removed and replaced with a slipper. All articles (such as money, watch, cufflinks) are removed from him. In this condition (and without a word of explanation), he is led into the Temple.

Organisation of a Lodge

While the candidate is being prepared by the Tyler in an anteroom, the officers of the Lodge will conduct a brief ceremony to 'open the Lodge in

---

[30] UGLE, *Constitutions*, 1984, Rule 162.
[31] 'A petitioner must be a man, in the full sense of the word, not a woman, or a child, or a eunuch.' Draffen, *Making of a Mason*, 27.

the First Degree'.[32] A minimum of seven officers must be present to conduct any business. There are nine regular officers: Worshipful Master, two Wardens, Treasurer, Secretary, two Deacons, Inner Guard, and the Tyler. The Master may also appoint men to other offices, such as Chaplain, Director of Ceremonies, Almoner, Organist, Assistant Secretary and Stewards – though no others.[33]

Though some Temples are elaborate and grand, the minimum furnishings of a Lodge meeting room are quite simple to provide, since the earliest meetings were in taverns. Even today, Lodges use large rooms above public houses or restaurants if they have no building of their own. The significance of the furnishings is explained to the candidate in a series of formal lectures, known as the 'Tracing Board'. There is a different one for each of the Degrees, their purpose being to act as visual aids to the moral lessons which the lectures contain.

Rituals ('Workings') of the Craft

Confusingly, although there are but three degrees in the Craft, there are four different titles awarded. According to the *Constitutions*:

> Pure antient [sic] Masonry consists of three degrees
> and no more, viz., those of the Entered Apprentice, the
> Fellow Craft and the Master Mason, including the
> Supreme Order of the Royal Arch.[34]

The precise wording and stagecraft of Masonic rituals varies in detail from place to place. According a Masonic historian, Dr David Harrison, there are around 50 different types of Craft rituals or workings in England alone, and if you include the working of individual Lodges, then there are countless variations.[35] Nevertheless, the structure of the Craft degrees is common to all its variations and the 'Landmarks' (particularly the various

---

[32] This and other Craft rituals are to be found in full in Walton Hannah, *Darkness Visible* (London: Britons Publ., 13th rev. ed. 1975), 83ff.

[33] UGLE, *Constitutions*, 1984, Rule 104a.

[34] This confusing statement is a compromise because of the 1813 merger of 'Antients' and 'Moderns'.
It meant that lodges could form 'Royal Arch' chapters, though these did not 'add' to the Three Degrees, but rather 'perfected' the degree of Master Mason.

[35] See dr-david-harrison.com (accessed 28 December 2020).

secret signs, grips and passwords) are consistently preserved, to enable one Mason to recognise another.

There was an attempt to standardise the rituals in England and Wales after the union of the 'Antients' and 'Moderns' in 1813. A 'Lodge of Reconciliation' was established to deal with disputes that arose from this process. In 1823, an 'Emulation Lodge of Improvement' was set up to establish and promote an 'authentic ritual' which was to be practised and learned, 'without permitting alteration'. Some Lodges resented this process.

For nearly a century, for example, there was an independent 'Grand Lodge of Wigan' which continued to practise the 'Antient' ritual. As a result of that 'Lancashire rebellion', Lodges were eventually allowed to regulate their own proceedings and their choice of working. Lodges began to use local variations, however, most of the Masonic workings in use today are variations of the original *Emulation* ritual, or 'working', even if a few Lodges remain defensive of their local version which forms part of their tradition. It was forbidden by Grand Lodge for the *Emulation* working to be printed, but variations of it developed through word-of-mouth and local custom. It was not published officially until 1969, by which time there had been many privately printed versions, each one differing from others and the later 'official version. Some versions began to be used in the later nineteenth century and, in a few cases, were sourced from pre-UGLE workings or using deliberately anachronistic language.

Today, workings may vary a little or be quite different in style from *Emulation* and gain their common Masonic name from an editor, publisher, or from part of a published title or its early place of use.[36] George *Claret* was a publisher of one of the earliest private versions, in 1833, having himself attended the Lodge of Reconciliation. In 1866, Malcolm Duncan published his 'Masonic Ritual and Monitor' in New York, thereafter known as *Duncan's*. During the 1880s, *West End, Logic* and *Oxford* workings were published, while *M.M. Taylor's* working of 1908, also known as *Hill's North London* working, and *Humber* and *Bottomley* also made an editorial choice to be quaint. In Scotland,

---

[36] A reason for bothering the reader with the names (in *italics*) of versions of these workings is that they are sometimes used as Masonic recognition ('dog whistle') words, being thought to be 'inaudible' to non-Masons.

Harvey's working is popular, being written out of concern of the non-Scottish elements that were entering the Scottish workings. Other Scottish workings include the *Standard, Modern, Goudielock* and *MacBride*. English examples are *Calver, Castle, Complete, Merchant Navy, Ritus Oxoniensis, Sussex, Thomas, Stability* (or *Standard, Muggeridge, Universal* and *Veritas*.) A helpful analogy here may be found in the public worship of the Church of England. There are mainstream liturgies, the *Book of Common Prayer* and *Common Worship*, which account for most public forms of worship but by no means all. Even within these more commonly used forms there is ample scope for local variation, as anyone who worshipped in different parish churches will know. So, it is with Masonic rituals.

Entered Apprentice

This is the First Degree, the one into which all Craft Freemasons are initiated. The preparation for this has been given. There are further questions about motives (along the same lines as the signed declaration) and frequent assurances of the piety, virtue and privileges of Freemasonry. An oath (called an 'Obligation') is taken which demands secrecy in unequivocal terms. As a further pledge of his fidelity a candidate is asked to seal his oath on the Volume of Sacred Law.[37] Only at this stage is his blindfold removed.

He is then taught the sign, grip and password of the Entered Apprentice.[38] It is also revealed to him, for the first time, that there are not one but 'several Degrees in Freemasonry, and peculiar secrets restricted to each'. He is exhorted to seek the 'aid and support of God his Creator' in his Masonic endeavours. A belief in God is considered by some to be a 'Landmark of Freemasonry', which is why the English Craft jurisdiction rejects 'fraternal relations' with any branch of Masonry that openly denies such a belief (for example, the Grand Orient Lodge of France).[39]

---

[37] In most Lodges of the UGLE this is a Bible. See the Glossary.

[38] These are given, along with those of other degrees, in Hannah, *Darkness Visible*, 82ff.

[39] J. S. M. Ward, *Entered Apprentice's Handbook* (London: Baskerville Press, n.d.), 61.

Fellowcraft

This is the Second Degree. It is assumed that every initiate will eventually reach the Third Degree and consequently this is a neglected ritual, despite the best endeavours of some Masonic commentators to boost it, for example:

> Herein is contained the Mystery not only of Masonry,
> but of all the religions, viz., the Union of Heaven and
> Earth and the Mediation between God and Man.[40]

The initiate is asked the question 'What is Freemasonry?', to which he is taught to reply.

> A peculiar system of Morality, veiled in Allegory, and
> illustrated by Symbols.[41]

This answer is hardly an explanation, even to an apprentice Mason. Once again, he is expected to prepare physically for the ritual, although this time he is not blindfolded, haltered or deprived of metals. There is another Obligation to be said, and a further sign, grip and password. The lecture of the second Tracing Board places emphasis on moral experience, education and fidelity. There is also clear indication that these render him acceptable to God:

> The Square teaches morality, the Level equality, and
> the Plumb Rule justness and uprightness of life and
> actions. Thus, by square conduct, level steps, and
> upright intentions we hope to ascend to those
> immortal mansions whence all goodness emanates.[42]

The pursuit of wisdom, as available through the natural sciences and liberal arts, is the highest endeavour of a Fellowcraft Mason. Thus equipped,

---

[40] J. S. M. Ward, *The Fellowcraft's Handbook*, (London: Baskerville Press, n.d.), Introduction.

[41] This is part of a 'catechism' a candidate must commit to memory prior to the Second Degree. Its significance will be discussed in the next chapter.

[42] Such a misunderstanding of the purpose and power of morality follows, of course, in the steps of Pelagius.

he need not shrink from toil nor will he faint beneath the heat and burden of the day, because his competency as a human being will be equal to the demands made upon him.[43]

Some considered this Degree to be an appeal for 'masonry of the mind' which will be a friend of enlightenment ... [and] become the enemy of bigotry or intolerance'.[44]

Master Mason

This is the Third and, in a sense, the highest degree of Freemasonry. Having been 'initiated' an Entered Apprentice, 'passed' a Fellowcraft, he is to be 'raised' a Master Mason. This is a reference to the central drama of the degree, which is said to be a 'dying and a raising [*sic*] again'.[45]

Once he has provided proofs of his status of Fellowcraft (in both signs and passwords) and, as with the previous two Degrees, the candidate retires to an anteroom to be prepared physically. The purpose of these requirements (being blindfold and haltered, with bare arms, breast and knees) is explained to him as follows: The hoodwink or blindfold that you wore represented the darkness before birth and education and also made it possible for you to be led from the Lodge Room without seeing it, if you refused to continue with the Ceremony. The cable tow placed around your neck was an emblem of the bondage which comes from ignorance, but together with the poignard which was presented to your naked left breast, also served to control your movements during the ceremony. You were divested of all metallic objects so that you could not bring any offensive weapons into the Lodge to disturb its harmony. The naked heel and the slipshod are because the ground is consecrated and the knee is bare so that there is nothing between it and the Earth when the Obligation is taken. The trouser leg is also rolled up to demonstrate the Candidate is a free man, bearing no marks of a

---

[43] From the 'Tracing Board Lecture of the Second Degree'; Hannah, *Darkness Visible*, 82ff.

[44] Draffen, *Making of a Mason*, 97.

[45] This clumsy term is perhaps used to emphasise the importance of those doing the 'raising'.

leg iron. The left breast is made bare so that the points of both the poignard and the compasses can be felt next to the heart and also to prove that the Candidate is not female... [46]

Another Obligation is required of him, this time sealed three times on the Volume of Sacred Law. In a highly charged atmosphere, perhaps to the accompaniment of Handel's 'Dead March' from *Saul* while someone reads from the Bible (often from Ecclesiastes 12), the candidate is lowered into a 'grave'. This may be printed on a sheet or woven in a carpet – or, dramatically, be a grave-trap in the floor, or even, in a few Lodges, a coffin.[47] Attempts to raise him by using the grips of the other two Degrees fail and the Worshipful Master commends the grip of a Master Mason, together with the 'Five Points of Fellowship'.[48] A new password is given and another Tracing Board lecture.

Great claims are made for the significance of this Degree:

> Here at length is the true purpose of Freemasonry: it is not merely a system of morality, veiled in allegory and illustrated by Symbols, but a great adventure, a search after that which was lost: in other words, the Mystic Quest, the craving of the Soul to comprehend the nature of God and to achieve union with Him.[49]

One writer clearly understood this degree to signify salvation:

---

[46] 'Explanation of the Symbolism of the Ceremony of Initiation'; https://www.pgldevonshire.org.uk/ (accessed 21 January 2021)

[47] This is part of a legend of Hiram Abiff, supposedly the builder of King Solomon's temple. See Glossary.

[48] The 'Five Points of Fellowship' are demonstrated and interpreted by the 'Worshipful Master' as he and the candidate embrace one another in this way: foot to foot (*service*); knee to knee (*prayer*); breast to breast (*secrecy*); hand to back (*support*); and cheek to cheek or mouth to ear (*counsel*). While in this position, the Worshipful Master then whispers 'Mah-Ha-Bone' into the ear of the candidate. Various meanings are given to this composite word, said to derive from an ancient Hebrew phrase – none of them is convincing.

[49] John S. M. Ward, *The Master Mason's Handbook* (London: Baskerville Press, n.d.), Preface.

> Among the manifold blessings that Freemasonry has
> conferred on mankind none is greater than that of
> taking the sting from death and robbing the grave of
> victory.[50]

The just 'wages' of a Mason who has proved himself, in the Three
Degrees, to be of the highest moral character is, 'the power to
comprehend the nature of God, who resides in the Master's Chair of the
Soul of every Mason'. Such knowledge has been won by his own
endeavours for, 'he cannot receive either more or less than he has
earned'.[51]

According to another Masonic commentator:

> the central teaching of the Master Degree ... [is] that
> there is a way for him to recover the possession of his
> own life, that he can be raised to a new manhood, lifted
> from the dead level ... to a living perpendicular ... By
> dying to his old life, by repudiating it, by finding again
> his faith in God – for the Power of God and the Power
> of the Brotherhood are there for him as much as for
> any other man – this is the path of his recovery.[52]

It must be remembered that there is no official interpretation of this or
any other Masonic degree.

Other degrees and orders[53]

A brief reference to the so-called 'higher' degrees is necessary here.
Perhaps fewer than a quarter of Craft Masons proceed through a variety
of other rituals.[54] Claims for these rites to form a part of Freemasonry rest
only on the requirement that their initiates must be Master Masons. The
Royal Arch Chapter is alone among these workings in being administered
as part of the Craft, though it is made clear that it is not a separate

---

[50] Ward, *Master Mason's Handbook*, Introduction.
[51] Ward, *Master Mason's Handbook*, 2.
[52] Draffen, *Making of a Mason*, 136–7.
[53] See Appendix II: Other Masonic Degrees/Orders.
[54] This is estimated from the membership claims of their respective websites and
journals.

degree.[55] This ritual involves a 'search' for a lost name of God which, when revealed to those who complete it, was found to be *Jah-Bul-On*.[56]

The 'Antient and Accepted Rite', known as the 'Scottish Rite' or 'Rose Croix', is popular with those who seek a 'Christian' element in Masonic ritual. Any Master Mason of twelve months' standing may apply for 'perfection' in the 'Rose Croix of Heredom' degree which, although being the 18th degree of this Rite, is the first that is 'worked', the others being conferred in name only. Here a Mason will be told, after yet another Obligation, that he is a member of a 'religious society', which is claimed by some members to be 'the perfection of Christianity'.[57] A commentary on this and other so-called Christian workings is found in Hannah's *Christian By Degrees*.[58] Today, some within the Craft consider these 'a bunch of rather secondary degrees which no-one else really wanted and which should have been allowed to die out', although this view is not held by all Masons.[59]

Notwithstanding their use of increasingly grandiose titles and elaborate rituals and regalia, the 'allied' Orders remain less important than the Craft Freemasonry degrees, mainly because to belong to any of them a man must have been 'raised' as a Master Mason.[60] However, reference to Appendix II, and to their respective websites will show that, after a lull in

---

[55] Bernard Jones, *Freemasons' Book of the Royal Arch* (London: Harrap, 1969), chs. 2–5.

[56] Walton Hannah, *Christian By Degrees* (London: Britons Publ., 4th ed. 1964). First used in eighteenth-century French Freemasonry, and later included in *Duncan's* working of 1866, some explain this revealed word as being a composite of Jahweh, Baal and Osiris; others that it was the name of an explorer from the time of Solomon. According to G. J. Midway, *Lure of the Sinister: The Unnatural History of Satanism* (New York: University Press, 2001), 259: 'In England, no ritual containing the name has been in official Masonic use since February 1989'. It is still used in the 'Rose Croix' rituals.

[57] In a conversation with the author in 1982.

[58] Hannah, *Darkness Visible*.

[59] See https://freemasonrymatters.co.uk/allied-masonic-degrees/degrees-of-significance/ (accessed 4 May 2020).

[60] For example, 'Knight of the Pelican and Eagle, the Sovereign Prince Rose Croix of Heredom' (18°, being a distinctive Masonic usage of geometrical shorthand, meaning 'Eighteenth Degree); 'Sublime Prince of the Royal Secret' (32°) and 'Sovereign Grand Inspector General' (33°), in the Rose Croix rituals.

the mid-twentieth century, there has been a growth in the number of esoteric Orders and to their membership in more recent times.[61]

It is in their rituals, perhaps even more than in their *Constitutions*, that the true nature of Freemasonry may be discerned. The effect on at least one Mason may be gained from this testimony:

> Now I went along, after some months, to be initiated as a Mason, and I had a vague idea what was going to happen, but I couldn't believe that my friend and his friends would indulge in the sort of spurious ceremonies that I'd heard about. Well, in fact, they did.[62]

What then is Freemasonry?

- **Morality?** Freemasonry is more than 'a system of morality, veiled in allegory' for many of its members.[63] In seeking to be 'all things to all men' it may have avoided dogmatic definitions of its religious character. Nonetheless, in broad terms, its constitutions and rituals owe more to the Enlightenment and the development of Rationalist thought than to any other claimed antecedents.
- **Brotherhood?** Freemasonry is a historic 'brotherhood' from which some men gain comfort. Institutionally it places an emphasis on secrecy, which it seeks to maintain by Obligations, sealed as oaths on the Bible. Freemasonry rejects the idea that it is a 'secret society', preferring to describe itself as 'a society with secrets'. That these Masonic 'secrets' (the signs, grips and passwords) are known outside of the Craft is beyond doubt.
- **Charity?** Freemasonry teaches the virtues of charity (which is generally understood to extend only to Masons and projects which

---

[61] Membership of all other degrees and orders is estimated, from their various websites and elsewhere, to be fewer than 45,000. In the Minutes of the 2017 Annual Meeting of the Grand Council of Allied Masonic Degrees (the largest grouping of 'higher' degrees), membership was said to have grown by 260 in the previous year.

[62] From an interview in the BBC TV programme 'The Open Secret', by James Dewar, broadcast 16 March 1965.

[63] Ward, *Master Mason's Handbook,* Introduction.

benefit them) and tolerance (which is interpreted to mean a deistic universalism). Discussion of religion and politics is formally forbidden within the Lodge, in the name of 'fraternal relations', which effectively prevents any departure from the Pelagian deist theology, established in their 'Antient Charges' of 1815.[64]

- **Christian?** The name of Christ is deliberately absent from all prayers offered to God by English Craft Freemasonry. This is to avoid criticism of 'sectarianism' (in Masonic terms this means being divisive because of one's religion). Despite this, Freemasonry provides both implicit and explicit assurances of eternal well-being to those who, as part of the Masonic brotherhood, lead lives devoted to morality and good works.[65]

- **Secret?** Freemasons consider investigation by any non-Masons to be an 'intrusion into their legitimate, and as they think their own, affairs'.[66] Nevertheless, there remain genuine areas of Christian concern about the tenets and practices of Freemasonry and these will be considered next.

---

[64] *Constitutions*, 9, Antient Charges VI, 'Of Behaviour'. 'Pelagian', followers of Pelagius (5th cent.) who taught the essential goodness of human nature, the freedom of human will, and the ability of a person to make themself acceptable to God by good works; 'deist', a believer in a god, without a name, as one who does not intervene in the universe.

[65] Church of England General Synod Report, *Freemasonry and Christianity: Are They Compatible?* 'GS Report (1987)'] (London: GS 784A, 1987), 34.

[66] Roger Lumley, 11th Earl of Scarbrough (UGLE Grand Master 1951–67), in a statement to the Press Association, 16 March 1965. Since 1984, with the publication of several leaflets by UGLE intended for public consumption and statements by Michael Higham (Grand Secretary 1980–98), the official attitude about secrecy may have changed in some measure; though Higham also wrote that, 'Freemasons would regret that such an inquiry is thought to be necessary', GS Report (1987), para 7.

3. CHRISTIAN RESPONSES TO FREEMASONRY

Roman Catholic

The Roman Catholic church has repeatedly condemned Freemasonry. Eight Popes since 1738 have issued warnings against it, supported by clear instructions to excommunicate any Catholic who chooses to remain a Freemason. What is not so well known is the extent to which the English Catholic hierarchy saw fit to accept Freemasonry in the 1970s.

Shortly after the beginning of Freemasonry, in 1738, Pope Clement XII indicated the following principal reasons why Masonic associations should be condemned from the Catholic, Christian, moral, political and social points of view:

- **Naturalistic philosophy**, through which was seen a strong appeal to religious relativism ('that religion in which all men agree') and a consequent contempt for orthodoxy and ecclesiastical authority.
- **Secrecy**, which he saw as a weapon for those who 'break as thieves into the house and like foxes endeavour to root up the vineyard'.[67]
- **Oaths and obligations** made to Freemasonry and Masonic work which, he believed, could not be justified in their scope, their object or their form, and consequently could not be held as binding upon an individual.
- **Civil and canonical law** could be threatened by such societies. Defence of Freemasonry by citing its good works would not remove the potential threat to the 'tranquillity of the State' and 'the spiritual health of souls' by a secret society based on a naturalistic philosophy.

Pope Leo XIII, in his encyclical *Humanum Genus*, 1884, observed the historical course of events 'demonstrated the prudence of our predecessors' (in condemning Freemasonry).[68] He saw the ultimate purpose of Freemasonry as 'the overthrow of the whole religious, political and social order based on Christian institutions' and its replacement with one founded on naturalism. The open anti-clericalism and avowed

---

[67] cf. Song of Songs 2:15 and Obadiah 1:5. The same metaphors that were used by Pope Leo X in his bull, *Exsurge Domine* (1520) against the teaching of Martin Luther.

[68] *Humanum Genus*, issued 20 April 1884. See the Bibliography.

atheism of French Freemasonry was cited as evidence for this view. It has remained the official Vatican view and was generally uncontested until the 1960s.

Masonic sources claimed that this uncompromising condemnation by the Roman Church during the time of Pope John XXIII (1958–63), and particularly following Vatican II, had been gradually softened.[69] Some credit is given by Masons to Ferrer Benimeli, who published a report showing that Craft Freemasonry did not, and should not, stand condemned under the papal bulls, because of its clear demand for a belief in God.[70] In France, 'a devoted French Catholic layman', Alec Mellor, obtained his priest's permission 'as a matter of conscience' to be initiated a Mason.[71]

It was in England that an even greater softening of Catholic attitude took place. Cardinal John Heenan was approached by Harry Carr, a Grand Lodge officer, with a view to a reconciliation between 'the Church and the Craft'.[72] Such was the rapport established that Heenan offered to act as an intermediary between the Vatican and the UGLE.[73] Heenan confidently expected the censure incurred for membership of Freemasonry to be abolished.[74] There followed 'several favourable signs [which] indicate that walls and fences are already being broken down'.[75] In contrast, the so-called 'Masonic Boom' in Italy in 1981, concerning corruption of the members of the so-called 'P2 Lodge', did little to help

---

[69] For example, Pick and Knight, *Pocket History,* 139; A. L. Philips, *Freemasonry for Beginners – and Others* (London: RMBI, 2nd ed. 1976), 83.

[70] J. A. Ferrer Benimeli, *La Masoneria despues del Concilio,* Spain, (1968); cited by Pick and Knight, *Pocket History,* 138. Benimeli was professor of Contemporary History at the Universidad de Zaragoza; though not a Freemason he is an acknowledged authority on the history of Freemasonry, especially in Spain and Latin America.

[71] Pick and Knight, *Pocket History,* 139.

[72] Heenan was Archbishop of Westminster (1963–75) and Harry Carr was an honorary Lodge member in 28 lodges in five countries. Carr was Assistant Grand Director of Ceremonies and later Junior Grand Deacon of UGLE.

[73] This rapprochement is described by Harry Carr, *The Freemason at Work* (London: the author, 6th ed. 1981).

[74] Archbishop of Westminster, *Ad Clerum,* 12 June 1973.

[75] Pick and Knight, *Pocket History,* 140.

international opinion of Freemasonry and eventually led to the downfall of the Italian government.[76]

That scandal did not seem to retard the developing goodwill between English Catholic hierarchy and Craft Freemasonry. In 1981, a spokesman for Cardinal Basil Hulme, Archbishop of Westminster, wrote in reply to a question about 'the official Catholic position' on Freemasonry:

> The present position is that we have been informed that Freemasonry in this country has no connection with the Freemasonry of an unpleasant kind on the Continent. Catholics who wish to join the Freemasons have to have permission from the local ordinary, who only gives it if he has been convinced that joining the Masons will not have any bad effect on the person's catholicity.[77]

The naivete of this reply was the more serious because of its source. It revealed that the English Catholic hierarchy had been 'informed' (by the Craft apparently) that, whereas political and atheistic European Freemasonry was 'unpleasant', in contrast, deist Craft Freemasonry was not.

Such a response was in marked contrast to the conclusion of the German Roman Catholic Bishops' Council, which published its report on its official discussions with German Freemasonry in 1980.[78] German Freemasonry has never exercised the same degree of secrecy as its English counterpart, though in most other respects it is similar. The

---

[76] The home of Lucio Gelli, Grand Master of the Propaganda Two (P2) Lodge, was raided by police. Afterwards a membership list of the P2 Lodge was published, revealing members of the armed forces, civil servants, bankers, industrialists and newspaper editors, many of whom had denied that they were Masons. Gelli was found guilty of fraud, arising from the collapse of the *Banco Ambrosiano*, which had close ties to the Vatican.

[77] Bishop David Norris, General Secretary to the Archbishop of Westminster, 8 December 1981, reply to Harry Carr, *Freemason at Work* (a copy of which was seen by the author).

[78] For details of the English translation of this report, see Bibliography. One of the authors of this report was Cardinal Joseph Ratzinger, later Pope Benedict XVI.

discussions had been conducted, since 1974, in 'a friendly atmosphere ... marked by frankness and objectivity'.[79]

The bishops observed that the fundamental doubt raised by the Roman Catholic Church about Freemasonry had not changed, which was that the objective validity of revealed truth in Christianity is repeatedly denied by Masonic indifferentism.[80] It went on to say that Freemasonry had not changed in its essence since the earliest papal bull, and that 'membership of it casts doubt upon the fundamental principles of Christian life'.[81] Their unequivocal and united conclusion was that:

> Membership of the Catholic Church cannot be reconciled with simultaneous membership of Freemasonry.[82]

The English Catholic hierarchy was brought back into line by the issue of a declaration from the Vatican's 'Sacred Congregation for the Doctrine of the Faith' in 1981. It reiterated the canon law which forbids Catholics, under the penalty of excommunication, to enrol in Masonic or other similar associations.[83] It went further by making it clear that:

> It was not, however, the intention of the Congregation to permit Episcopal Conferences to issue public pronouncements by way of a judgment of a general character on the nature of Masonic associations, which would imply a derogation from the aforesaid norms.[84]

So much for an 'English exception' to the Vatican's historic ban.

---

[79] German Bishops' report, *Zur Frage der Mitgliedschaft von Katholiken in der Freimaurerei* (Mainz: Kirkheim, 1980). See Bibliography for details of the English translation.

[80] German Bishops' Report, Part 3 (ii).

[81] German Bishops' Report, Part 3 (iv).

[82] Statement of the German Bishops' Council, 12 May 1980.

[83] *Code of Canon Law*, 2335.

[84] From the Office of the Sacred Congregation for the Doctrine of the Faith, 17 February 1981, signed by Cardinal Franjo Seper.
https://www.vatican.va/roman_curia/congregations/cfaith/documents/rc_con_cfaith_doc_19810217_massoni_en.html (accessed 22 January 2021).

Nonconformists

Protestants have never been consistently and clearly against Freemasonry. A disclosure and condemnation written from a Methodist viewpoint was published in the 1920s and resulted in a resolution being passed at Methodist Conference condemning Freemasonry.[85] Nevertheless, some Lodges continue to have strong Methodist connections.[86] Various polemical booklets have been written by those from a Presbyterian tradition, largely based on older, inaccurate, disclosures.[87]

More thorough research has sometimes been limited in its effect by a narrow critical framework.[88] Such writers frequently confuse the various types Freemasonry. Their conclusions have done little to convince Christians outside their own theological persuasion. An exception to this, perhaps, was by the international mission director, Oswald Sanders.[89]

Church of Scotland

A report of the Church of Scotland on Freemasonry was published in 1965. Its Panel on Doctrine had been given this brief:

> Investigate the issues involved in Church members who are under vows to Christ, being members also of societies involving secret ceremonies and secret binding oaths.[90]

---

[85] Charles Penney Hunt, *The Menace of Freemasonry to the Christian Faith* (Nottingham: Freedom Press, 1927).

[86] For example, the so-called 'Epworth Lodges'; Pick and Knight, *Pocket History*, 130.

[87] For example, W. J. M. McCormick, *Christ, The Christian and Freemasonry* (Edinburgh: the author, 1977).

[88] For example, James Payne, *The Christian, The Word of God, and Freemasonry* (London: Sovereign Grace Advent Testimony, 1964) which concluded that 'Higher Criticism, the New Theology, Modernism, Barthianism etc. are but products of Masonry', 38.

[89] J. Oswald Sanders, *Cults and Isms* (London: Lakeland, 1978). Sanders (1902–92) was general director of China Inland Mission.

[90] Church of Scotland, report by the Panel of Doctrine, *Freemasonry and the Taking of Oaths*, 1965.

It concluded that Freemasonry was not a religion, though some of its members regarded it as such and that secrecy, of itself, is morally neutral meaning that secrets could only be condemned if they were found to be contrary to Christian doctrine. The Panel decided that it was important to remind Masons that those who were also members of the church has a prior claim made upon them by Christ but stopped short of an outright condemnation. Some of the Panel asked to include this additional comment:

> It appears that the initiate (Freemason) is required to commit himself to Masonry in the way that a Christian should only commit himself to Christ.[91]

Church of England

By far the most significant critique of Freemasonry in the twentieth century was that by Walton Hannah.[92] His short article about Freemasonry in an academic journal in January 1951 caused considerable disquiet.[93]

It might have done little more than that had not the press magnate Lord Beaverbrook allowed his dislike of the Archbishop of Canterbury, Geoffrey Fisher (a known Freemason), to be voiced through the *Daily Express* and so make a 'scandal' out of it.[94] As a result, the subject was debated in the Church Assembly in June 1951, when a Masonic royal chaplain, Ralph Meredith, proposed that a commission be appointed to report on Hannah's article.

Hannah's contention had been that Freemasonry was a modern form of Gnosticism (a claim to possess a 'higher' or 'inner' knowledge of God that

---

[91] Church of Scotland Report, 9.

[92] A Church of England vicar, Hannah subsequently left the Church of England to become a Roman Catholic priest in Montreal, Canada. See Bibliography for details of his books and articles.

[93] Walton Hannah, 'Should a Christian by a Freemason?', Theology 54, (January 1951): 3–10..

[94] Max Aitken, 1st Baron Beaverbrook (1879–1964); Calderwood, Paul, *Freemasonry and the Press in the Twentieth Century: A National Newspaper Study of England and Wales* (London: Routledge, 2016), *The Daily Express*, 15 January 1951, cited as footnote 56

is available only to a few) and that it exercised a parasitic influence within the church through its appeal to syncretistic universalism and a naturalistic philosophy. Yet in the Church Assembly debate, Hannah's theological arguments were ignored. Meredith said that there had been an unwarranted attack on a 'brotherhood of princes, prelates and peers, and a great body of ordinary men'.[95] He defended Freemasonry as:

> A brotherhood which seeks after truth, encourages members to uphold one another in the highest moral principles and in strict honesty of purpose and integrity in all matters of business.[96]

One speaker described Freemasonry as 'one of the greatest factors in the building of modern civilisation' and, along with other clerical Masons present, declared that it was impossible for a non-Mason to speak authoritatively about Freemasonry, saying 'You cannot understand Freemasonry except in a Lodge'.[97] This argument was particularly successful in discrediting Hannah's objections to Freemasonry.[98] The debate effectively ended when the Archbishop of York, Dr Cyril Garbett, said:

> Freemasonry in this country has always avoided anti-clericalism which makes it offensive on the Continent. It has never made any attack on Christianity and the Church ... I am reassured (turning to Archbishop Fisher) by your Grace's being a member of the Order and by the fact that a distinguished layman, Lord Scarbrough, is Grand Master of the Order.[99]

The Assembly rejected the proposal (with only one vote against), a result that Meredith admitted he welcomed and for which he had hoped.

In response, Hannah published a book to prove that the claimed secrecy of Freemasonry was a myth and that 'respectable' English Freemasonry had much in it to concern Christians. He was cogent in his arguments

---

[95] Pick and Knight, *Pocket History*, 130.

[96] Pick and Knight, *Pocket History*, 130.

[97] Pick and Knight, *Pocket History*, 131.

[98] Hannah was never invited to defend his case, but instead watched the debate from a public gallery.

[99] Pick and Knight, *Pocket History*, 131.

and extremely thorough in his research. Years later he was able to write to another researcher on the subject:

> What I did not print was that I myself have visited Masonic Lodges, have witnessed the conferring of all three degrees, plus the Royal Arch ... and so successfully had I decoded the secrets that I have never been caught as a gate-crashing non-mason.[100]

So successful was Hannah's critique of Masonic oaths and obligations that severe disquiet was expressed by several senior Masons. By 1961, this was even admitted by 'the world's premier Masonic research Lodge':

> During recent years there have been many strong representations made against the retention of the barbarous penalties in the various Obligations, all of which are wholly impracticable in present-day society. The criticism is well founded.[101]

In 1964, the subject was debated by the UGLE, at the best attended meeting in living memory, and it was resolved by Bishop Percy Herbert, the Masonic Provincial Grand Master of Norfolk.[102] He proposed a change of wording in the Obligations for the benefit of those who were

---

[100] James Dewar, 'The Open Secret', 105. During the 1987 General Synod debate, Dr Margaret Hewitt, chair of the Working Group, quoted the opinion of UGLE's Grand Secretary (Michael Higham) regarding Hannah's work – that it was 'unfortunately accurate'.

[101] Harry Carr, 'The Obligation and its Place in the Ritual', *Ars Quatuor Coronatorum*, LXXIV (London: Quatuor Coronati Lodge, 1961). This Lodge's claim to Masonic research pre-eminence is still made on their website (https://www.quatuorcoronati.com, accessed 28 December 2020); also that their Lodge was 'consecrated' in 1886.

[102] Bishop of Norwich (1942–59).

troubled by the 'barbarous penalties'.[103] This proposal was accepted and subsequently adopted by many Lodges.[104]

In 1979, the UGLE Grand Master, the Duke of Kent, expressed further misgivings about the physical penalties, which were still being widely used within other Craft rituals. He raised the matter again in 1985. After debate in June 1986, UGLE finally resolved that:

> All references to physical penalties be omitted from the Obligations taken by a Candidate in the three Degrees and by a Master Elect at his Installation but retained elsewhere in the respective ceremonies.[105]

Church of England clergy

Since the 1950s there has been a considerable decline in the number of Church of England clergy who are Freemasons.[106] The last archbishop to be a Mason was Geoffrey Fisher. When, as a student in 1959, Kenneth Leech had the temerity to ask the archbishop, 'Is it possible to be a Christian and a Freemason?', Fisher replied, 'Yes, because I am', whereupon his fellow students booed Fisher for his reply.[107] Three years later Leech asked a similar question of Fisher's successor, Michael Ramsay, who said, 'I'm never quite sure how seriously to take it, but I think it is ridic, ridic, yes, ridiculous!'[108]

---

[103] Effectively, the change was from 'beware of this penalty' to 'remember what used to be the penalty'. There is no evidence that the 'barbarous' penalties had ever been enforced.

[104] His seconder was the ubiquitous Harry Carr, for whom the revised wording must have gone some way towards helping his discussions with the Archbishop of Westminster.

[105] GS Report (1987), Appendix VIII.

[106] Soon after he was consecrated in 1959, Mervyn Stockwood, Bishop of Southwark, claimed that he was one of only two diocesan bishops who was *not* a Freemason. This was probably an exaggeration, but it is indicative of the strength of Freemasonry in the episcopacy at the time. In the late 1940s, the Craft could perhaps claim a membership of 1 in 17 of all men in the UK; today it is more like 1 in 170.

[107] Letter from the Revd Dr Kenneth Leech to *Church Times*, 8 June 2011.

[108] Leech to *Church Times*, 8 June 2011.

Robert Foxcroft, a former chaplain to the Royal Masonic Hospital, questioned the secrecy of Freemasonry in a BBC radio programme in 1980. He wanted to know whether the Masonic benefits to society (which they claimed) 'outweigh the liability of a movement which provokes such widespread, if ill-founded, suspicion.' [109] He later went on to be even more dismissive of the Craft, which he termed 'the mafia of the mediocre'.[110]

A survey was conducted in 1981, by a TV programme, '*Credo*', which sent a questionnaire about Freemasonry to the 145 bishops in the Church of England.[111] Some 35 (24%) refused to comment or failed to reply, 104 (71.2%) denied that they were Masons; of these 61 (42%) indicated that they had serious misgivings about Freemasonry to the extent that they would want to restrict the content of Masonic services held in churches. Only six, some of whom were retired, admitted to being Masons.

Michael Marshall, Bishop of Woolwich, echoed some of the concerns of the German bishops. When interviewed for '*Credo*', he said, 'There is nothing more ugly, I think, than a self-made man who worships his maker.'[112] For him, Freemasonry clearly taught a gospel of works whereas 'the whole centre of Christianity is that a man cannot be justified by good works'.[113] He also objected to what he saw as the elitism of Freemasonry, which he considered to be in contrast to the Christian gospel and the biblical doctrine of humanity, he said, 'I am most human, as a Christian, when I relate to the whole of humanity.'[114]

A generation after the abortive Church Assembly debate in 1951, there was clearly a different climate of opinion among many Church of England clergy. A General Synod debate on Freemasonry in 1987 would attempt to establish this beyond doubt.

---

[109] Robert Foxcroft, 'On The Square', BBC Radio 4; subsequently published in *The Listener*, 24 April 1980, 525.
[110] In a conversation with the author, in 1982.
[111] '*Credo*: Christ and Freemasonry' (London Weekend Television, 1981).
[112] '*Credo*' (LWT, 1981).
[113] Michael Marshall, cited by Clifford Longley, 'Masons and the Church: a storm coming?', *The Times*, 2 July 1981, 12.
[114] *Credo*: Christ and Freemasonry' (LWT, 1981).

4. General Synod and Freemasonry

In February 1985, the General Synod passed a private member's motion moved by Roderick Clark, a lay representative of the Diocese of Lincoln:

> That this Synod requests the Standing Committee to bring forward for debate a report which considers the compatibility or otherwise of Freemasonry with Christianity.[115]

There was an unexplained delay by the Standing Committee in responding to this motion. The satirical magazine *Private Eye* speculated whether this could be because the general secretary of General Synod, Derek Pattinson, was himself a Freemason.[116] The reason given in the Report of the Working Group, eventually published in June 1987, was that the election of a new General Synod had been the cause of the delay.[117]

The inclusion of two declared Masons in the working group, Peter Moore, Dean of St Albans, and Ronald Hart of Exeter, meant that the Report was not open to the objection of it being written entirely by 'ignorant' non-Masons.[118] While preferring not to go as far as other members of the working group, these Masons concluded that 'there are clear difficulties to be faced by Christians who are Freemasons'.[119]

Upon examining the various Masonic rituals, the group found that, despite unprecedented co-operation by the UGLE, Masonic secrecy was

---

[115] General Synod Working Group report, *Freemasonry and Christianity: are they compatible?* (London: Church House Publishing, GS 784A, 1987), para 1 ['GS Report (1987)'].

[116] The author of this book was also the author of that article in *Private Eye*. A briefing paper, based on the Working Group's Report, was also prepared by this author for circulation to Synod members. Derek Pattinson (who was later knighted and ordained) was secretary general of General Synod from 1972–90.

[117] GS Report (1987), para 4.

[118] Other members of the General Synod Working Group were Dr Margaret Hewitt (Chair), Dr Christina Baxter, the Rev. John C. Broadhurst, Rev. James C. Duxbury and Rev. David R. J. Holloway.

[119] GS Report (1987), para 122.

still a significant cause for concern. Claims that Freemasonry is a 'private' rather than a 'secret' society were not accepted.[120] The Report also concluded that much-publicised revision of the wording of the Masonic oaths 'does not and cannot wholly meet all criticism of the Obligations'.[121] Acknowledging that some men have never felt any incompatibility between their faith and their Freemasonry, the group concluded that the rituals 'can only be a grave embarrassment to Freemasonry and a very powerful basis for its critics'.[122]

The Working Group was 'at one in rejecting the assertion that the rituals of the Craft contain no element of worship.'[123] There is an assurance of eternal well-being and of a salvation by works expressed implicitly and explicitly within these rituals. The charitable good works done by many Masons still appear 'to have the marks of a familiar English heresy – Pelagianism – since the grace and forgiveness of God in Christ and the power of the Holy Spirit are being ignored'.[124]

Understandably, in view of their original brief (and the constraints imposed on them by a small budget and just five meetings), the Report asked more questions than it answered. An important question was raised, 'Is Freemasonry in fact and effect a religion?', to which there was no clear response. The Report did point out a contradiction in some Masons' claims: since discussion of religion and politics within the Lodge meetings are expressly forbidden by the Constitutions, this would seem to exclude the opportunities for evangelism that had been claimed by some Masonic Christians.[125]

The Report acknowledged that Christians reject gnostic claims of further 'revelation' (a feature of the Holy Royal Arch ritual) beyond that found in Christ. Furthermore, the Report concluded that the word JAH-BUL-ON, whether as a name or a description of God, used in some rituals, must be considered 'blasphemous'.[126]

---

[120] GS Report (1987), para 106.
[121] GS Report (1987), para 54.
[122] GS Report (1987), para 91.
[123] GS Report (1987), para 110.
[124] GS Report (1987), para 100.
[125] GS Report (1987), para 109
[126] GS Report (1987), 91.

The Report was sent to every member of Synod and, at the same time, a copy of the evidence submitted to the Group by the United Grand Lodge of England was also sent, though this was at the instigation and expense of Grand Lodge.[127] The two documents arrived at about the same time and therefore invited comparison. The Masonic document was extensive, thoroughly indexed and clearly presented, which could not be said of the Working Group's Report. Skilful presentation could not obscure the fact that the reason for Grand Lodge distributing their evidence was because they did not like the conclusions reached by the Working Group.

During its July 1987 sessions, General Synod met to consider whether to endorse the Report. The motion before the Synod was straightforward: the Working Group wanted the Report to be 'received and commended for reflection within the Church'. For a while, the issue being debated seemed to be whether Freemasons were 'good people'. What seemed to be overlooked was the fundamental question faced by the Working Group: are the Christian gospel and Freemasonry *compatible*?

The Archbishop of York, Dr John Habgood, said that he regarded Freemasonry as 'fairly harmless'. He thought that Synod was treating the whole subject too seriously by commissioning the Report in the first place. To use words like 'heresy' and 'blasphemy' was, he said, to judge Freemasonry by inappropriate standards. As for Masonic rituals, 'these are harmless pleasures', he concluded.[128]

The Bishop of Manchester, Stanley Booth-Clibborn, said 'secrecy can be fun, but it can lead to misunderstanding on both sides'.[129] He urged that there should be no undue pressure brought to bear on Masons, many of whom were among 'the best Christians in the churches', to leave the Craft. The issue here was not whether secrecy was right, but to what use was it being put.[130]

---

[127] *Evidence on the compatibility of Freemasonry and Christianity* (London: UGLE, 1986).

[128] Clifford Longley, 'Criticisms of Masonry Endorsed', *Church Times*, 17 July 1987, 20.

[129] *Church Times*, 17 July 1987, 20.

[130] The subject of secrecy was especially topical in 1987, in the wake of the publication of the book *Spycatcher* by a former MI5 agent. The British Government had sought to prevent its publication. The argument of the

Dr Christina Baxter was the first to call unequivocally for the Report to be received, in the terms of the motion, and without amendment. She used the biblical account of the woman caught in adultery to establish both the need for forgiveness of the sinner and for the abhorrence of the sin. She saw two questions raised by the Report:

- Why have we taken so long about warning people about things which might spoil their relationship with God?
- And why have we failed to offer men the fun, fellowship and enjoyment they find in Freemasonry?[131]

Dr John Sentamu also wanted the motion approved without amendments.[132] He commented that many of the Masonic rituals seemed like the 'pagan rituals' he had used before he became a Christian. If Jesus was the finality, then to what extent should a Christian engage in such rituals, he wondered? One amendment was passed, with the approval of the chair of the Working Group. The words 'reflection within' were strengthened to 'discussion by' the church.

When this revised motion was put to the Synod, the motion was received by 394 to 54 against, with just five abstentions. This showed that Synod wanted the subject to be discussed throughout the Church of England, because it shared the concerns expressed in the Report that there are serious causes for thinking Christianity and the Craft are incompatible.

In the decades since, open support for Freemasonry among Church of England clergy has dwindled. The last diocesan bishop to admit being a Mason was William ('Bill') Westwood, Bishop of Peterborough, who died in 1999. Nevertheless, in 2005, Professor Dianne Kirby still found that 'perceptions of the Church of England as a traditional stronghold of Freemasonry persist'.[133] This was confirmed in 2007, when John Hamill, UGLE Director of Communications, was reported to have said,

---

publishers was that some secrets need to be revealed for the public good to ensure that the security services remained free from corruption.

[131] *Church Times*, 17 July 1987, 20.

[132] The Rev Dr John Sentamu, at the time of the debate was a parish priest, later becoming Archbishop of York.

[133] Dianne Kirby, 'Christianity and Freemasonry: the compatibility debate within the Church of England', *Journal of Religious History*, 29:1, February 2005, 43–66 (accessed 6 May 2020).

Today, except in relation to the evangelical wing of the Church, relations are much happier and freemasons – individually and as a group – are again welcome in the Anglican Church.[134]

Yet it remains the case that, from a Masonic point of view, it 'is being slowly muscled out of the British social picture' and that this 'will, in turn, affect the morale of Freemasonry worldwide'.[135]

An academic survey conducted in 2011 assessed the views on Freemasonry held by senior clergy (not including bishops) through a qualitative survey that attracted 518 responses (a response rate of 64%). The survey generated more negative responses about Freemasonry than positive responses, although these were based, it concluded, 'on personal contact, hearsay, and anecdote, rather than on an informed examination of the issues'.[136]

In 2011, Jonathan Baker, who had been chosen to be the Bishop of Ebbsfleet, was revealed to be a Mason.[137] After it was made public, Baker agreed to resign from his Masonic membership, though not because he thought it incompatible with his faith.

> Had I ever encountered anything in freemasonry incompatible with my Christian faith I would, of course, have resigned at once. On the contrary, freemasonry is a secular organisation, wholly supportive of faith, and not an alternative to, or substitute for it. In terms of the Church of England, its

---

[134] Tobias Churton, *Freemasonry – The Reality* (Lewis Masonic, 2007/9), 505–06.

[135] Churton, *Freemasonry – The Reality*, 528.

[136] Tania ap Siôn, Leslie J. Francis and Caroline Windsor, 'How Anglican Clergy Perceive Freemasonry: Complementary System, Incompatible Enemy or Harmless Eccentricity?', *Journal of Contemporary Religion* (2011) 26:2, 225–243 (accessed 6 May 2020).

[137] See *Daily Telegraph*, 14 May 2011; Ebbsfleet is a non-geographical bishopric, created in 1994 to provide episcopal oversight to clergy who did not agree with the ordination of women.

support, for example, for cathedral fabric is well documented.[138]

Support for the fabric may account for why cathedrals are among the few places in the Church of England to continue to offer a public affirmation of Freemasonry. In December 2012, for example, the dean of St Albans, Jeffrey John, welcomed some 800 Hertfordshire Masons, in their regalia, to a service of thanksgiving and rededication of a pulpit which had been a Masonic gift in 1883.[139]

According to provincial Masonic websites, in 2017, to celebrate the tercentenary of Craft Freemasonry, Masons in regalia paraded at services in other English cathedrals including Canterbury, Chelmsford, Exeter, Lincoln, Manchester, Peterborough, Salisbury, Truro, Wells and Winchester, and have done so since in Durham, Gloucester and Guildford. In response to a question about these services tabled at General Synod in 2018, Christopher Cocksworth, Bishop of Coventry, referred to the 1987 Synod report and 'added that cathedral services were required under canon law not to contravene church doctrine.'[140]

---

[138] George Conger, http://anglican.ink/2015/06/25/ (accessed 30 April 2020).
[139] https://www.freemasonrytoday.com/ (accessed 7 May 2020).
[140] Harriet Sherwood, *The Guardian*, 8 February 2018, 'C of E raises serious concerns about Christian Freemasons' (accessed 5 October 2020).

5. Areas of Christian Concern

What may we learn from the attitude of the Christian church to Freemasonry during the past three hundred years? Its criticism has been sporadic and its praise sparse. At times, Freemasonry has been regarded as a threat to the church and, at others, as a benign influence in the morality of men. What has been consistent is that there are some areas of real concern of which Christians of any tradition should be aware. With some contrivance admittedly, these form a recognisable acronym:

Fatherhood of God
Real fellowship
Ecumenism and tolerance
Equals Pelagianism
Masonic religiosity
Attitude to the Bible
Son of God
Oaths and obligations
Not free to leave?
Right use of secrecy
Yet for Christians...

Fatherhood of God

'Great Architect of the Universe' is the title Freemasons use for God in their rituals and ceremonies. It is a deliberately quasi-secular term, with its origin in the teleological arguments of the early eighteenth-century and is like the 'celestial watch-maker' kind of analogy. It affirms, by implication, that God who has 'designed' the universe is now effectively absent from it; as a watchmaker parts with a watch that has been made, so an architect hands over the responsibility for any building that has been designed.

Christians believe that God has taken the initiative and revealed his names in the Scriptures, and through them we may learn something of God's character. The revelation of Jesus Christ is that God is the creator and sustainer of all that there is, and is also a personal God, who deals with us as a father deals with his children. The Christian gospel is that, through the merits of Jesus Christ, we may dare to call him 'Father'. Such intimacy is absent from Masonic titles for God, perhaps because it implies a continuing relationship.

Real fellowship

Fellowship of the church of Christ is eclectic and inclusive. This stands in marked contrast to the 'universal brotherhood' of Freemasonry. Founded on a principle of exclusiveness (only men, and not even all of them, may belong), its fellowship may well seem genuine to its members, though from a Christian viewpoint, it is sadly counterfeit. Likewise, Christian charity is, ideally, unbounded. Naturally, Christians often fall short of the ideal. But Christians claim a divine reality – acceptance by God – which makes genuine love available to all. Without this reality, it is hard to see what can transform our basically selfish nature.

A Freemason is expected to extend his charity within the brotherhood, but then only 'so far as may fairly be done without detriment to myself or my connections'.[141] Less charity is expected of a Mason to those who are outside of the Craft, while to those who pretend to be Masons, 'You are to reject (them) with contempt and derision and beware of giving ... any hints of knowledge'.[142]

Freemasons speak of being 'on the level' or 'on the square' with one another (that is, equal in fellowship) and yet clearly have a highly developed structure of rank and privilege. With few exceptions a Freemason is dependent upon being wealthy for advancement within the Craft.[143] These are not the criteria which Jesus taught for those who would know true fellowship.

---

[141] From the Obligation recited by a candidate as part of the Tracing Board lecture of the Third Degree, that of Master Mason.
[142] *Constitutions*, no. 6.
[143] This assertion is made because of the cost of lodge (or lodges) subscriptions, literature and regalia, as well as the hospitable and charitable expectations, which inevitably increase with a person's status within Masonry. Exceptions may be made to those who have noble titles or those whose membership, it may be thought, would bring lustre to the Craft in some other way.

Ecumenism and tolerance

One of the principal tenets of Freemasonry is that of tolerance. Where creeds, dogma and, for that matter, politics are concerned, the official line is 'live and let live'. That this is effectively a deliberate indifferentism is denied:

> We do not mean that one belief is as true as another, or as valuable as another ... but we know that the truth can never emerge unless each man is left free to see the facts for himself ... Let each human mind have a fair deal; let it be free to observe the world for itself. This, we believe, is the one way in which the truth about any of the great subjects of human life will ever be found.[144]

The Masonic author here argues that Freemasonry is founded on a naturalistic philosophy (that is, that we can, through reason and the natural sciences, comprehend eternal truth). Christians reject this, claiming that only in God's revealed will, supremely in Christ, may eternal truth be known. Tolerance in Freemasonry is therefore different in character from, for example, Christian ecumenism. Freemasonry implies that truth may be found apart from Christ, while Christian ecumenism fundamentally affirms and holds central that Christ is *the* truth.

Equals Pelagianism

Probably the most widespread misunderstanding of Christian doctrine is that someone can, by what they do, make themselves acceptable to God. Christian orthodoxy identifies this problem as Pelagianism, which in many disguises down the centuries has passed for true Christian faith.

The Reformation re-established what had been a biblical doctrine from the very beginning: that a person can be justified before God by faith alone, and that even that faith is an unmerited gift of God.[145] For a Christian, any system of morality which purports to make a person

---

[144] Draffen, *Making of a Mason*, 68.
[145] See Ephesians 2:7–9.

morally acceptable in God's sight and that is not grounded in an active faith in Christ, can have no foundation in truth.

Masonic religiosity

Craft Freemasonry has recognised that the relationship of Masonry and religion is of fundamental importance to the reputation and well-being of English Freemasonry. For some Masonic writers, the position in clear: 'it cannot be too strongly asserted that Masonry is neither a religion nor a substitute for religion'.[146] The problem is whether such a statement, however clearly it may be worded, changes the actual practices of Freemasonry. It may be argued that the Masonic rituals are but harmless moral allegories, based on the Old Testament, which were never intended to be a substitute for faith. However, such an interpretation is impossible for the ritual of the Holy Royal Arch and other Allied Degrees. A 'secret' which is revealed to some Masons is the 'last name of God' – and it is certainly not the Holy Trinity as understood by Christians. The whole of Masonic literature is full of religious language and though this may not constitute a separate religion it is certainly steeped in religiosity – which is an extremely poor substitute for real faith.

Attitude to the Bible

Christianity is fundamentally a religion of revelation, holding that God is both self-revealing and self-authenticating (cf. John 8:13-18). The Masonic attitude to revelation is that belief in any revelation is a matter for personal decision and relative to the faith one may hold; in which case no revelation, Christian or otherwise, can make an absolute claim to be true.

This means that the Bible must compete on equal terms with the various 'holy books' of the world's major religions.[147] For some Freemasons, the Bible is their Volume of Sacred Law, useful for the sealing of oaths, but discussion of its contents within the Lodge is expressly forbidden. To do so would be deemed to be 'sectarian'. This means all truth becomes 'relative' and Christian doctrine (which includes any understanding of the Bible as the revealed Word of God) must thereby be only one of the ways in which we may comprehend God.

---

[146] Draffen, *Making of a Mason,* 69.

[147] Freemasonry has seven recognised 'Volumes of Sacred Law'; cf. Charles J. Carter, *The Director of Ceremonies* (Shepperton: Lewis Masonic, 1989), 71.

Son of God

The cornerstone of the Christian faith is the divine person and work of Jesus Christ. Christians believe that in the person of Christ they may know God as he truly is. Christ is the Word of God made flesh, the perfect expression of God to humanity.

For this reason, Christianity rejects the idea that there could be a 'higher knowledge' of God than that which is found in Jesus Christ. This would be a form of Gnosticism, which the church since earliest times has repeatedly rejected. The Masonic claim to be able, through the working of their rituals, to impart 'light' to a candidate is therefore empty for a Christian, because those rituals are not focused on Christ and indeed Craft Freemasonry rituals make no mention of Christ. Even the faintest hint that Christ is incidental rather than essential for salvation is clearly unacceptable to a Christian. Yet the Tracing Board lectures (given during the Masonic initiations) make no reference to Christ and yet still offer an assurance of eternal well-being.

Oaths and obligations

The oaths and obligations of Freemasonry have been the most regular source of criticism by the church. Despite the 'permissive penalties' being introduced, a number of difficulties remain.[148] Yet these oaths in effect make it no simple matter for a conscientious man to withdraw from the Craft. The oaths are made 'before God' and without 'evasion, equivocation, or mental reservation of any kind'.[149] So according to one Masonic writer, 'It would be impossible for a man to take a more sacred and binding vow, and he who could be false to it necessarily is morally corrupt at the centre of his being.'[150] Furthermore, according to the *Constitutions* of Freemasonry, 'It is not in the power of any Man or Body of Men to make innovation in the Body of Masonry.'[151]

---

[148] Although the 'physical penalties' have, since 1986, been moved from the Obligations in the Craft degrees, they have not been removed entirely but form part of a lecture given by the Worshipful Master to a newly initiated candidate.
[149] From the 'Oath and Obligation of a Master Mason'.
[150] Draffen, *Making of a Mason*, 42–43.
[151] *Constitutions*, vii, no. 11.

Though some Christian traditions have disagreed, it is not generally held that the taking of an oath before God is contrary to Scripture. Yet, as one ancient phrase has it, 'vain and rash swearing is forbidden Christian men.'[152] Either the oaths that Freemasons take are meant seriously, in which case they constitute 'rash swearing', or they are not – in which case it is 'vain swearing' and are equally unacceptable for a Christian.

Not free to leave?

The penalties that once formed part of the oaths of Freemasonry may never have been enforced, yet there are genuine constraints on Masons to discourage them from leaving. From the testimony of many current and former Masons these would seem to be of the following character:

- **Social**: A man cannot become a Mason unless recommended by two existing Masons. At least one, possibly both, will be a close friend or family member, whose reputation within the Craft is affected if the man they recommend eventually dislikes Freemasonry, or is disliked by it. A long-standing Mason may have few friends outside of the Craft. He may feel that he puts many friendships at risk if he resigns.
- **Moral**: The careful screening of a man to ensure that he is not a 'stupid atheist nor an irreligious libertine',[153] and the comprehensive nature of the oaths (sealed on a 'Volume of Sacred Law' which, at least nominally, the initiate believes to be sacred) means that a Christian man who wishes to leave the Craft may believe himself to be in a moral dilemma. He is prevented from discussing the oaths with any non-Mason by the terms of the oaths themselves. He may think, quite wrongly, that they are morally binding upon him.
- **Financial**: As a man progresses within the Craft, so he will be more committed financially. In addition to the Lodge fees, there are the numerous often expensive social functions. There is also an increasing awareness that his commitment to Freemasonry is measured, to a large extent, by his giving to Masonic charities. A Mason may well have shown more financial commitment to the

---

[152] Article XXXIX in Thirty-Nine Articles of the Church of England. cf. Matthew 5:33–37.
[153] *Constitutions*, 'Charges of a Freemason', no. 1.

Craft than to any other cause, his church included. It is not easy for a man to admit he may have wasted so much money.

- **Physical**: The dreadful mutilations which are threatened in the penalties, are clearly no more than 'gothick' melodrama. Yet, in a sense, there is another quite genuine physical penalty. A 'respectable' man is obliged to submit to the physical preparations for each Degree. Any sense of bewilderment or shame he may feel is countered by his friends assuring him that they too have been through it. A major consequence of these preparations is to inhibit a man from speaking openly about the Craft, for fear of ridicule and embarrassment.

Right use of secrecy

Secrecy is not prohibited by Christian ethics and indeed Christ himself made use of it for a time.[154] Christian charity, business ethics, a state's security, the law of the land, and common sense all demand some aspects of secrecy of particular people at times. Nevertheless, secrecy may be used and demanded in a way that is contrary to Scripture. Secrecy itself may be understood as morally neutral, but the secrets themselves are not. There are right and wrong secrets and hence a right and a wrong use of secrecy. A Christian would want to be quite sure that at least the foundation of Freemasonry, the 'Antient Landmarks of Freemasonry', were in accordance with Christian doctrine before swearing an oath of secrecy to protect them.

Yet for Christians...

To Freemasons, criticism may be unwelcome and seem unwarranted. From a purely humanitarian perspective, Freemasonry probably does little harm and even some good. The key issue is not what Freemasonry claims to be, or even if it does good, but what it is when measured against the gospel. Notwithstanding the occasional Masonic scandals, few would doubt the good works and even the high motives of many Masons. Yet for Christians that is not enough.

---

[154] cf. Matthew 16:20.

6. Some Pastoral Guidelines

What is to be the approach when you learn that someone you know is a Freemason? What can you say to someone who has been asked to become one? What would you reply to a request by the local lodge to use your church for a Masonic service? What follow are some guidelines, drawn from the experience of Christian ministers who have had to answer such questions.

The movement and the man

It is especially important to distinguish between the two. Your opinions about Freemasonry are one thing. Your attitude to individual Masons is another. It is not unusual for a non-Mason to have great apprehension, even fear, about the supposed influence of Freemasonry. There is no reason to release that fear on the first genuine Freemason that you come across.

Freemasons are usually men who think of themselves as morally good (they are encouraged by the Craft to do so). It is likely to come as a shock to them if you suggest otherwise. Remember, you are on sensitive ground. Personal feelings, indeed, even identity, will be at stake if a Freemason discusses his commitment to the Craft, or admits to any shortcomings in it.

Having read this book, you may know more about Freemasonry than many, possibly most, Masons. If the Mason you meet is a newly initiated 'Entered Apprentice' he will barely have heard of the Holy Royal Arch, let alone be able to discuss the significance of the composite 'lost Name of God'. Try to discern the level of experience and commitment to Freemasonry that a Mason may have.[155] Do not use a pastoral 'sledgehammer to crack a walnut'.

Commitment and conversion

It has been observed that the English are typically deist (that is, believing in a god without defining that belief too clearly, for fear of offending

---

[155] The Mason you meet may well be a 'Country Member', a term that the Craft uses of someone who, having once been an active member (in regular attendance and dues paid) has let his membership lapse.

anyone else). If that is so, then the typical Freemason is a Pelagian deist – that is, he is taught to believe that he is making himself acceptable to this largely unknown god by the system of morality inculcated in the Craft and the good works that he does.

Such a man may be in your church and may well be one of the most active members. But commitment without conversion can be a dangerous thing, for two reasons. First, the commitment shown by an unconverted man will be for motives other than the love of God in Christ. This will inevitably lead, in time, to the establishment of priorities at variance with the gospel. Secondly, he may wrongly believe himself to be acceptable before God by his own efforts.

C. S. Lewis provided an analogy for this kind of person's predicament from a Christian point of view.[156] Imagine you are standing at the top of a cliff overlooking a village where your home is. You may be so close to the village that, if your position were to be marked on a map, it would seem just a short walk to the village. Yet suppose you are unable to descend that cliff safely. Another person, who had turned round and taken a longer path to the village would be *nearer by approach* during most of their journey – even though you, who remained standing by the cliff edge, would be *nearer by distance*.

So it is, Lewis observed, that good people, by their own efforts, are judged by the world to be nearer to heaven, the 'village' of the story, although it is the one who has chosen the true path (that of Jesus Christ) who alone can be certain that they will one day arrive.

But what may be said to the man who holds to a clear Christian faith and yet still chooses to remain as a Mason? Be patient with him. Consider his motives for membership and the constraints against his leaving. Ask yourself if resigning would be an easy decision for him to make. If you have the opportunity, speak of your own experience of the love of God in Christ, and especially of the richness of God's grace – of a love that we cannot earn.

Motives for membership

What kind of reasons motivate a man to want to join? An understanding of these will help in your counsel, particularly potential Candidates for

---

[156] C. S. Lewis, *The Four Loves* (London: Geoffrey Bles, 1960; 1991 ed.), 5–6.

Initiation. The following constitute the more common reasons given, gained from conversations with Masons and ex-Masons.

- **Social:** A man may find himself the only one of his peer group who is not a Mason. It may be the 'done thing' by certain groups (such as Old Boys' Lodges associated with some schools). An otherwise shy man may find that he can mix freely in a group of like-minded men. The clearly defined authority structure with corresponding social roles appeals to many men. This may explain the many lodges with military and police connections.

- **Ambition:** It may be suggested to a man that his career prospects would be improved if he joined Freemasonry, even if Grand Lodge clearly rejects such suggestions. A Mason is charged only 'to prefer a poor brother that is a good man and true before any other poor people in the same circumstances'.[157] Yet it seems that Masonic 'brotherhood' is no stronger than many other 'networks' in our society.

- **Security:** Having heard something of Masonic benevolence, at least towards Masons and their families, a man may consider the Craft to be little more than a broad form of insurance against hard times. Providing a Mason regularly pays his dues, he is unlikely to be disappointed on his own behalf, although some evidence of dissatisfaction among Masonic widows was found.[158]

- **Philanthropy:** There is no doubt that some men are moved towards membership by the Craft's reputation for generosity. Regular lists of all donations are published to members by Grand Lodge and larger sums are mentioned in Masonic year books.

- **Spiritual:** Despite any official protestations to the contrary, many men find a kind of spiritual satisfaction within the rituals of Freemasonry. These are, for the most part, dignified (with the obvious exception of the initiations) and disciplined. They have some claim to antiquity and within any one Lodge are rarely subjected to revision. Familiarity brings its own comfort, especially to older men who may adapt to radical changes in later in life only with reluctance.

---

[157] *Constitutions of the Antient Fraternity of Free and Accepted Masons* (London: UGLE, 2016), 150.

[158] It is possible, of course, that it is only the discontented Masonic widows who want to talk to non-Masons.

- **Identity:** A man who in all other respects may feel himself to be a 'nobody' may discover a sense of his own worth within the Lodge. The grandiose titles, the regalia, the respect for Lodge officers and eventually the respect commanded within the Craft, may all appeal to a man, especially if he has a sense of failure or poor achievement in other areas of his life.

- **Mystery:** Although at one level the secret Masonic rituals may be dismissed as childish charades, at another they obviously appeal to those with a need for mystery. Such a need is not surprising in a society which has lost a genuine sense of the transcendent and replaced it with either arid rationalism or fearful superstition. What can be questioned is the extent to which Freemasonry, lacking any genuine mystery, continues to require unwarranted oaths of secrecy instead.

- **Elitism:** This is clearly part of the appeal of Freemasonry. There is a distinction, albeit a fine one, between the person who by circumstance or achievement is a member of a group others consider to be elite and the person who desires to join such a group. Its aim is towards a goal which, if attained, finds more satisfaction in those whom it rejects than in those whom it permits to belong. Such a desire is harmful to moral character and must eventually end in frustration.

- **Pressure:** A son of a Mason, when eligible to become a member (at the age of 21 years), may well find that he comes under pressure to join from his father. He is likely to know little or nothing about the Craft and to be quite unable to provide reasoned objections. Apart from such close family pressure there is little evidence to establish actual coercion as a reason for membership.

Hard questions for the church

An examination of the appeal to men of Masonic brotherhood obliges us to consider the ways in which the church may have failed him. A glance at the 'Motives for Membership' above may well reveal some of the shortcomings of the Christian fellowship which he has known. A few questions will help to make clear what this means:

- **Fellowship:** Does he have the healthy fellowship of other men of his own age in the church? Or is it, like so many, attended largely by women?

- **Authority:** Are his abilities suitably used? Or is the minister the only person with any real authority in the church?
- **Assurance:** What assurance, both temporal and eternal, has been offered to him?
- **Practical:** Have there been practical examples of a caring love for families in need, and clear teaching on the Christian fellowship, which is the right of every child of God?
- **Vision:** Is there a concern for the needs of the world beyond the local church doorstep? Does that care take the form of regular giving of time and money?
- **Expectancy:** Is there a sense of divine expectancy in worship? Or is more time spent in church services in 'finding the right page of the service book than in finding God'.[159]
- **Self-worth:** Do men feel worthless (rather than unworthy) through poor teaching of the gospel? It is then understandable that some would look for ways to please God. Without opportunities for rewarding service within the church, then they will look elsewhere.

These are hard questions to face, but entirely relevant to the problem of deciding a pastoral response to organisations like Freemasonry. If there are serious shortcomings within a church, it is not surprising that men should look towards a counterfeit fellowship, such as the Craft, to fulfil their needs. It was wisely observed that 'where the church neglects a duty, a sect develops'.[160]

---

[159] A remark made by Dr Gerald Bray, when teaching doctrine to students at Oak Hill College.
[160] Attributed to Ronald Knox (1888–1957), by his sister-in-law, Mary Knox, in a conversation with the author but a printed source has not been found.

Appendix I: Masonic Abbreviations

There were few abbreviations used in early Masonic printed works. There are none in Anderson's *Constitutions* (1723), for example. Since the early twentieth century, printed rituals are full of abbreviations, to prevent non-Masons from knowing key words and terms. Here are some of them:

∴   Used as an elision in place of an ellipsis ('...'), perhaps a reference to a triangle (as formed by a geometrical compass)

A&AR/AASR	Ancient & Accepted Rite (Scottish Rite = the 'Christian' Degrees)
AF&AM	Ancient Free & Accepted Masons
AMD	Allied Masonic Degrees (see Appendix II)
AQC	*Ars Quatuor Coronatorum* (a journal of Masonic research)
ARU	Architect and Ruler of the Universe (from the MM degree, a Masonic term for God)
AYM	Ancient York Masons [North American rites]
Bro	Brother
CH/COH	Captain of the Host (Royal Arch)
Comp	Companion (Royal Arch)/Compasses
D	Deacon
EA	Entered Apprentice (First Degree of Craft Freemasonry)
EC	Excellent Companion (Royal Arch) or English Constitution
EHP	Excellent High Priest
F&AM/FAAM	Free & Accepted Masons
FC	Fellowcraft or Fellow Craft (Second Degree of Craft Freemasonry)
FPF	Five Points of Fellowship
GAOTU	Great Architect of the Universe (from EA degree, main Masonic term for God)
GGOTU	Grand Geometrician of the Universe (from FC degree, another Masonic term for God)
GL	Grand Lodge
GM	Grand Master
GOF	Grand Orient of France

GS	Grand Secretary/Grand Scribe
HA	Hiram Abiff
HP	High Priest (Royal Arch)
HRA	Holy Royal Arch
IGH	Inspector General Honorary (A&AR 33°)
IM	Illustrious Master
IPR	Initiation, Passing, and Raising (progress through the three Craft Degrees)
JD/S/W	Junior Deacon/Steward/Warden
K	King (Royal Arch)
KS	King Solomon
L	Level
MC	Master of Ceremonies
ME/C/M	Most Excellent/Companion/Master
MIGM	Most Illustrious Grand Master
MM	Mark Master/Master Mason (Third Degree of Craft Freemason)
MW/B	Most Worshipful/Brother
PGM/PM	Past Grand Master/Past Master
PR	Plumb Rule
PS	Principal Sojourner (Royal Arch)
PW	Password
RA	Royal Arch
RAM	Royal Arch Mason/Masonry or Royal Ark Mariner
RE	Right Excellent
RW/B	Right Worshipful/Brother
S	Scribe (Royal Arch) or Senior
Sq	Square
SD/S/W	Senior Deacon/Steward/Warden
TBL	Tracing Board Lecture
TIM	Thrice Illustrious Master
T	Triangle
QC	Quatuor Coronati Lodge, London (a Lodge for Masonic research)
UD	Under Dispensation
UGLE	United Grand Lodge of England
VSL	Volume of Sacred Law
VW	Very Worshipful
WB/M	Worshipful Brother/Master

APPENDIX II: OTHER MASONIC DEGREES/ORDERS

KEY

- Orders in regular text admit all faiths
- Orders in *italics* admit only Trinitarian Christians
- Candidates may have to fulfil other entry requirements
- Year is of last establishment of an Order in UK or Eire
- The Order and Fraternity of Women Freemasons are separate from Craft Freemasonry and its Allied Orders
- Information sourced from the websites of the Orders and layout adapted from charts on Wikiwand.com

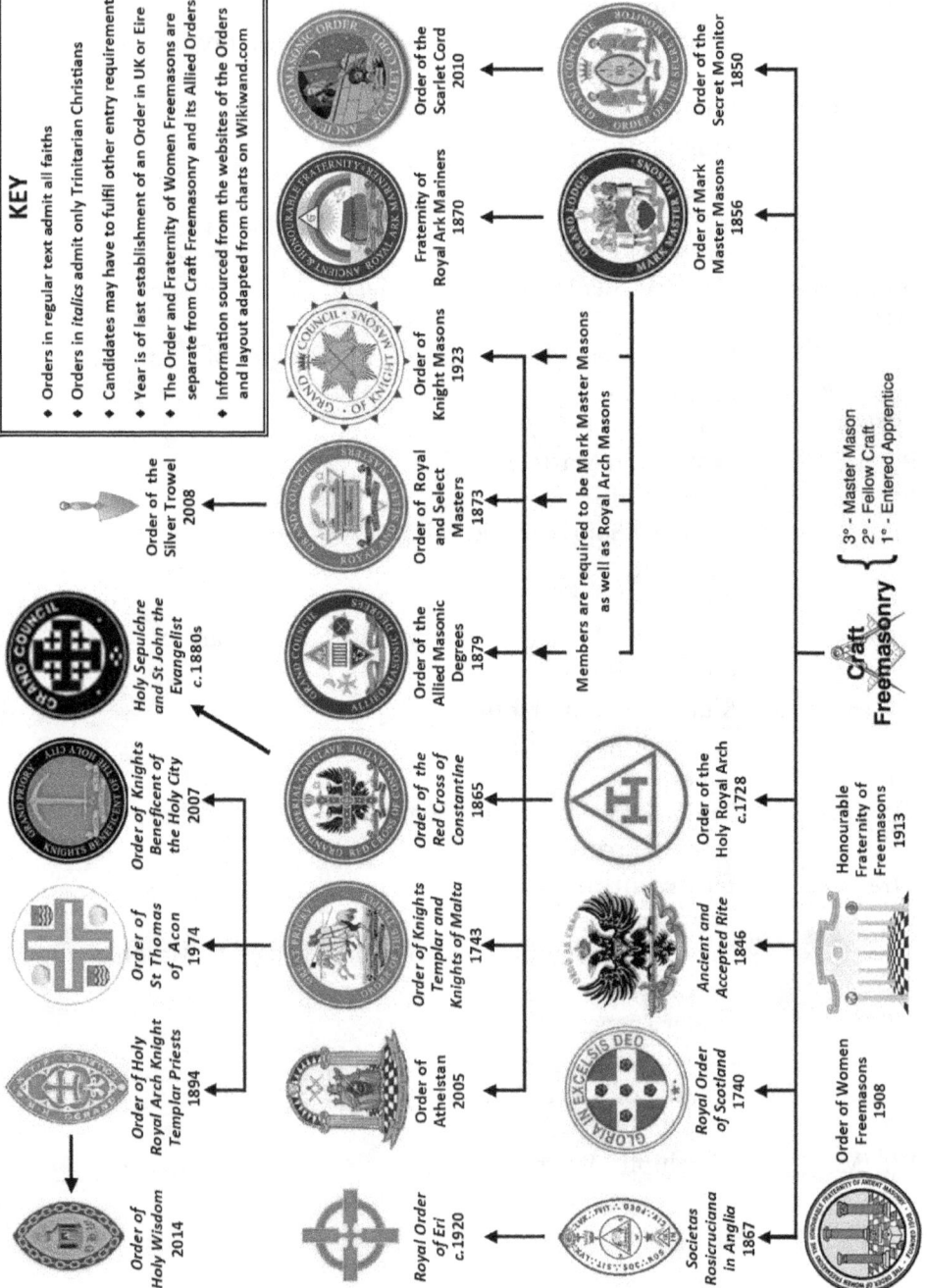

Order of the Scarlet Cord 2010

Order of the Secret Monitor 1850

Fraternity of Royal Ark Mariners 1870

Order of Mark Master Masons 1856

Order of Knight Masons 1923

Order of Royal and Select Masters 1873

Members are required to be Mark Master Masons as well as Royal Arch Masons

Order of the Silver Trowel 2008

Order of the Allied Masonic Degrees 1879

Holy Sepulchre and St John the Evangelist c.1880s

Order of Knights Beneficent of the Holy City 2007

Order of the Red Cross of Constantine 1865

Order of the Holy Royal Arch c.1728

Order of St Thomas of Acon 1974

Order of Knights Templar and Knights of Malta 1743

Ancient and Accepted Rite 1846

Honourable Fraternity of Freemasons 1913

Order of Holy Royal Arch Knight Templar Priests 1894

Order of Athelstan 2005

Royal Order of Scotland 1740

Order of Women Freemasons 1908

Craft Freemasonry

3° - Master Mason
2° - Fellow Craft
1° - Entered Apprentice

Order of Holy Wisdom 2014

Royal Order of Eri c.1920

Societas Rosicruciana in Anglia 1867

Appendix III: Glossary of Masonic Terms

Allied Degrees: Beyond Craft Freemasonry, there is wonderland of rituals and **Lodges** to which a Master Mason may aspire. See Appendix II.

Antient Landmarks: The fixed and unalterable principles of Freemasonry. Every Master on attaining the Chair of the **Lodge** vows to uphold and maintain them. Grand Lodge is unable by the *Constitutions* even to discuss their alteration. However, other than the signs, handgrips and passwords, no one within the **Craft** knows precisely what the **Landmarks** are. There have been many suggestions made but there is no official definition.

Cowan: A term, adopted from Scottish **Operative** Masonry, meaning 'non-Mason'.

Craft: A collective noun for Freemasons. Strictly, it refers only to Three Degrees, as used by UGLE and other Grand Lodges in 'harmony' with it.

Degree: One of the three stages of initiation on the way to becoming a Master Mason, and any subsequent ritual within Freemasonry.

Grand Orient: The name of one kind of French Freemasonry, which is an example of an avowedly atheistic type, and therefore not in 'harmony' with the UGLE.

Hiram Abiff: The central character that features in the Third Degree. Supposedly the builder of Solomon's Temple and said to have been murdered. This story is given a moral significance, some even going so far as to suggest he was a forerunner of Christ.

Lewis: A Masonic symbol of a cramp iron derived from **operative** Masonry and used to denote a young man adopted by a **Lodge** or a recent member.

Lodge: Like the word 'church', this word can be used to mean the people or the place in which they meet. A 'regular' Lodge is one constituted by UGLE and has at least seven members.

Operatives: A term used by Freemasons to describe those who work in stone, from whom they borrowed the name of their **Craft**.

Passwords for each **Degree:** 1) Entered Apprentice – 'Boaz'; 2) Fellowcraft – 'Shibboleth' and 'Jachin'; 3) Master Mason – 'Tubal Cain' and 'Mah-Ha-Bone'.

Speculatives: those, such as Craft Freemasons, who do not work with stone but who use the tools and skills of **Operative** masons in a philosophical or symbolic way as metaphors for living a good life.

Tyler (or Tiler): In speculative or symbolic masonry, a Master Mason whose duty it is to challenge all who enter a Lodge to ascertain that they are Masons who are duly qualified.

Working: A Masonic term for their rituals. Thus Freemasons 'work' the Three Degrees rather than 'use' or 'recite' them. It is used when discussing various versions of the rituals.

Volume Of Sacred Law: This is placed on what Masonic rituals refer to as a 'pedestal' and many Masonic commentators refer to as an 'altar'. Rather revealingly, Masonic rituals also refer to the 'VSL' as 'furniture'.

Bibliography

Because of the challenge of gathering reliable information about Freemasonry, this bibliography has been amplified beyond the information usually given to include a personal comment about the value of some of the materials used for this study and, where available, a British Library shelf mark is given as [...], or a webpage where the text may be found.

By Masonic authors

Bailey, Foster, *The Spirit of Masonry* (Tunbridge Wells: Lucis Press, 1957)
'Masonry is a spiritual quest', the author asserts. A thorough treatment of this approach. Full of statements that would embarrass Freemasons who wish to minimise the religious aspects of Craft rituals and practice. [4787.b.17]

Beha, Ernest, *A Comprehensive Dictionary of Freemasonry* (London: Arco, 1962)
For 'discerning Masons who wish to know the facts about the institution to which they belong'. Useful. [3111.d.45]

Brown, Arthur, *The Fourth Gospel and the Eighteenth Degree* (London: Rockliff, 1956)
'The first book to interpret any Masonic degree from an exclusively Christian standpoint'. An oblique reply to the criticisms raised in Hannah's second book, *Christian by Degrees.* [3228.ee.3]

Calderwood, Paul, *Freemasonry and the Press in the Twentieth Century: A National Newspaper Study of England and Wales* (London: Routledge, 2016).
The Secretary of a Lodge of Masonic research explores, through newspaper reports, why the Craft went from being widely admired in 1900 to its low ebb a century later. [DRT ELD.DS.59009]

Carr, Harry, *The Freemason at Work* (London: the author, 6th ed., 1981).
A reliable and informative work, although inevitably somewhat dated. [X.429/14135]

Carter, Charles J., *The Director of Ceremonies* (Shepperton: Lewis Masonic, 1989)
> A handbook to assist in the planning of Masonic rituals. [YK.1993.a.192]

Castells, Francis de, *Genuine Secrets of Freemasonry prior to AD 1717* (London: A. Lewis, 1930).
> The author is entirely convinced that Freemasonry is descended from Jewish Kabbalism. Considerably more invention than information. [366.1*1547*DSC]

Churton, Tobias, *Freemasonry – The Reality* (Hersham, Surrey: Lewis Masonic, 2007)
> Founder-editor of the magazine, *Freemasonry Today,* and lecturer at Exeter University. 'Jesus redefined the temple, and this definition is at the heart of Freemasonry'. A useful overview from the viewpoint of a contemporary gnostic. [YC.2009.a.11858]

Constitutions *of the Antient Fraternity of Free and Accepted Masons* (London: UGLE, 2016)
> The rulebook of Craft Freemasonry. Minor details revised every few years. Given to a candidate when initiated into the First Degree. ex-Masons. [Anderson's 1723 ed., republ. 1976; X.205/526;] https://www.ugle.org.uk/images/files/Book_of_Constitutions_-_Craft_Rules_Sept_2017.pdf

Draffen, George, *The Making of a Mason* (London: A. Lewis, 1978)
> An introduction to Freemasonry by an authoritative writer. [X.529/21432]

Gould, Robert F., *The History of Freemasonry* (London: Caxton, 3rd ed., 1951)
> A *magnum opus* of research first published 1888. Not essential reading. [04784.i.19]

Hamill, John M., *The Craft: a History of English Freemasonry* (Wellingborough: Crucible, 1986)

A history of the Craft by the then Librarian of UGLE and curator of the Freemasons' Hall museum, London. Obviously authoritative. [YH.1986.a.196]

Heindel, Max, *Freemasonry and Catholicism* (London: L. N. Fowler, 9th ed., 1978)
Rosicrucian claims to outline the 'cosmic facts underlying these two great institutions as determined by occult investigation'. A waste of paper. [X3/8776 DSC]

Horne, Alex, *King Solomon's Temple in the Masonic Tradition* (London: Aquarian Press, 1972)
An American, 'hoping to arouse a deeper understanding and appreciation of Freemasonry in the light of biblical, historical and mythological traditions': what is lacking from the first two of these is insufficiently compensated by the third. [72/3745 DSC]

Hughan, William J., *Masonic Sketches and Reprints* (London: G. Kenning, 1871–79).
1: 'History of Freemasonry in York', 2: 'Unpublished Records of the Craft', 3: 'The old charges of British Freemasons', 4: 'Memorials of the Masonic Union of A.D. 1813', 5: 'A numerical and statistical register of Lodges which formed the United Grand Lodge of England'. Several useful source documents in one volume. [4784.f.6]

Jones, Bernard E., *Freemasons' Guide and Compendium* (London: Harrap, 1959)
Thorough, accurate and authoritative – and tedious. [W34/1253 DSC]

Jones, Bernard E., *Freemasons' Book of the Royal Arch* (London: Harrap, 1969)
'The Ineffable Name', the principal quest of this ritual, remains unmentioned and unexplained. Of limited interest. [X.102/393]

Lawrence, John, *Masonic Jurisprudence* (London: A. Lewis, 3rd ed., 1923)

Includes a list of Grand Lodge decisions on matters great and small – mostly small – from 1813–1922. The author is not to be confused with a much later Christian writer on Freemasonry. Same name, different reasons for writing. [04782.f.31]

Lennhoff, Eugen, *The Freemasons* (London: A. Lewis, 1978)
An English translation of a German classic history of the Craft first published in 1934. A useful survey of the development of European Freemasonry. [366.1 *3079*DSC]

Mellor, Alex, *Histoire Des Scandales Maconniques* (Paris: Belfond, 1982)
A survey of the *affaires célèbres* of Freemasonry from the 18th century to the 'P2 Lodge' scandal of 1980. [F11-6461 DSC]

Philips, A. L., *Freemasonry for Beginners – and Others* (London: RMBI, 2nd ed., 1976)
Some useful information. [Privately printed, not in British Library]

Pick, Fred L., and Knight, Gilfred N., *The Pocket History of Freemasonry* (London: F. Muller, 7th ed., 1983).
A reliable source of 'orthodox' Masonic opinion. [83/08329 DSC]

Redman, Graham, *Emulation Working Today* (London: Lewis Masonic, 2007)
Full workings of a Craft Lodge from one tradition. Key words and phrases are printed by initial letter only. Minimal crossword skill (or a copy of *Darkness Visible*) are needed to decode it. Understanding the point of it will take longer. [YK.2009.a.36016]

Prichard, Samuel, *Masonry Dissected: being a universal and genuine description of all its branches from the original to this present time* (London: J. Wilford, 1730)
The earliest authentic exposure of the Craft practices by an ex-Mason. [RB.23.a.17789]

Robbins, Alfred, *English-Speaking Freemasonry* (London: Ernest Benn, 1930)

A useful account of the history leading up to the UGLE.
[04784.de.73]

United Grand Lodge of England, *Masonic Year Book*, London, UGLE
Useful statistics of new membership and Lodges with record of
major Masonic events in recent years. [Current editions available
only through UGLE to presumed Masons.]

UGLE, *Freemasonry and Christianity : evidence on the compatibility of
Freemasonry and Christianity* (London: UGLE, 1986).
A glossy defence published to coincide with the General Synod
debate in 1987. [YC.1988.a.6663]

Ward, John S. M., *The Entered Apprentice's Handbook* (London:
Baskerville Press, n.d.)
Ward, John S. M., *The Fellowcraft's Handbook* (London: Baskerville
Press, n.d.)
Ward, John S. M., *The Master Mason's Handbook* (London: Baskerville
Press, n.d.)
Ward, John S. M., *The Higher Degrees Handbook* (London: Baskerville
Press, n.d.)
Popular mystical commentaries by an eccentric author, first
published without date in the early 1920s and reprinted many
times since. Disavowed by UGLE in 1987, more recently these
books have been published as a combined volume with the title,
'*The Scholar the Builders Rejected ... '* (Calgary, Canada:
Theophania Publ., 2011). [Not found in the British Library but
full text of the first title may be found at:
http://www.freemasons-
freemasonry.com/ward_EA_handbook.html with links from
there to the text of the other titles, accessed 28 December 2020.]

By non-Masonic authors
Carlile, Richard, *Manual of Freemasonry, in three parts ...* (London, the
author, 1845)
A detailed and accurate exposé of the texts used by Craft
Freemasons at the time that has been used by the Craft since to
fill gaps in their historic records. [W22/5162 DSC]

Church of England, *Freemasonry and Christianity* (London: General Synod, 1987)
> Prepared by the working group established by the General Synod in the light of the motion carried by the General Synod in February 1985. It was overwhelmingly endorsed after the eventual debate. [YC.1988.a.930]

Church of Scotland, *The Church and Freemasonry* (Edinburgh: St Andrew, 1990)
> Makes fine theological distinctions that are not always convincing and concludes that Freemasonry is incompatible with Christianity. [YC.1990.a.4686]

Dewar, James, *The Unlocked Secret – Freemasonry Examined* (London: Corgi, rev. ed., 1990)
> Thoroughly researched, written and well-illustrated. One of the best books by a non-Mason written without a religious perspective. [YK.1992.a.1758]

Dillon, George F., *Grand Orient Freemasonry unmasked as the secret power behind Communism ...* (London: Britons Publ., 5th ed., 1965).
> Roman Catholic interpretation of the effect of Freemasonry on European history first published in 1885. Shows its age. [X.100/2383]

Finney, Charles G., *Character and Claims of Freemasonry* (Hanley: Tentmaker, rev. ed., 1996)
> A passionate plea by an ex-Mason for others to avoid the Craft, first published in 1868. [YC.2000.a.2861]

Fraser, Hamish, *Freemasonry and The Church: are they compatible?* (Saltcoats: the author, 1973)
> A traditionalist Roman Catholic response to Cardinal Heenan's *Ad Clerum* of 12 June 1973. [Not in British Library]

Foxcroft, Robert, 'Brotherhood of Man', *The Listener*, 24 April 1980.
> An account of the experiences of a non-Mason, ex-chaplain to the Royal Masonic Hospital, who was researching for a radio programme about Freemasonry. [5275.700000 DSC]

Hannah, Walton, 'Should a Christian be a Freemason?', *Theology* 54, January 1951

The article that eventually prompted the later books by the same author. [Not found in British Library, but facsimiles for sale at https://journals.sagepub.com/doi/pdf/10.1177/0040571X5105436702, accessed 28 December 2020]

Hannah, Walton, *Darkness Visible* (London: Britons Publ., 13th rev. ed., 1975)
Contains the most thorough disclosure of Craft rituals available. Cogent objections from a Christian point of view. [76/42656 DSC]

Hannah, Walton, *Christian By Degrees* (London: Britons Publ., 4th ed., 1964)
Equally thorough discussion of the Allied Degrees, including those purporting to be Christian in content. [X.100/665]

Hunt, Charles Penney, *The Menace of Freemasonry to the Christian Faith* (Nottingham: Freedom Press, 1927)
Stirred a debate among Methodists in England. [04784.de.32].

Jacob, Margaret C., *The Radical Enlightenment: Pantheists, Freemasons and Republicans* (London: Allen & Unwin, 1981)
Interesting account of the origins of European Freemasonry from a social historian's viewpoint. An appendix includes a copy of the Masonic *Constitutions* of 1723. [X.809/48122]

Kirby, Dianne, 'Christianity and Freemasonry: the compatibility debate within the Church of England', *Journal of Religious History* 29:1 (2005), 43–66.
This article uses primary sources from Lambeth Palace to explore in detail the 1950s debate, when the compatibility question involved King George VI and the Archbishop of Canterbury, Geoffrey Fisher.

Knight, Stephen, *The Brotherhood – The Secret World of the Freemasons* (London: Granada 1983)
A book responsible for bringing the subject of Freemasonry back into public debate in Britain. Concerned primarily with Masonic corruption in society, it did not spare the blushes of the Church of England. Its inaccuracies are neither as many nor as serious as the UGLE claimed. [V83/33791 DSC]

Lawrence, John, *Freemasonry – a way of salvation?* (Bramcote: Grove Pastoral, 10, 3rd ed. 1988)
> Pastoral rather than persuasively didactic. [X.529/49348]

Lawrence, John, *Freemasonry – a religion?* (Eastbourne: Kingsway, 1991)
> Useful and pastoral. [YK.1992.a.1896]

Leo XIII, Pope, *Humanum Genus*, Encyclical on Freemasonry (Vatican, 1884)
> A thorough discussion of some of the theological problems involved. [Not in British Library, but full English text found at: http://www.vatican.va/content/leo-xiii/en/encyclicals/documents/hf_l-xiii_enc_18840420_humanum-genus.html, accessed 28 December 2020]

McCormick, William J.M., *Christ, The Christian and Freemasonry* (Edinburgh: the author, 1977)
> A Presbyterian polemic against Freemasonry with considerable confusion between the various Masonic traditions. [X.100/17501]

Payne, James, *The Christian, The Word of God, and Freemasonry* (London, Sovereign Grace Advent Testimony, 1964)
> Written from Presbyterian viewpoint with a limited bibliography; dated (first published 1943), with no essential insight. [X.108/1091]

Rainsbury, Albert W. ('Bertie'), *Freemasonry: of God or the Devil?* (Croydon: the author, 1959)
> A sermon preached in Emmanuel Church, South Croydon, relying heavily on Walton Hannah's research. Significant because it was a pioneering publication, on the cusp of a change of attitude within the Church of England. [Not in British Library, but text available at: https://www.christianstudylibrary.org/article/freemasonry, accessed 28 December 2020]

Sanders, J. Oswald, *Cults and Isms* (London: Lakeland, rev. ed., 1962)
> A chapter is concerned with American Freemasonry. [W57/7492 DSC]

Siôn, Tania ap, Leslie J. Francis and Caroline Windsor, 'How Anglican Clergy Perceive Freemasonry: Complementary System, Incompatible

Enemy or Harmless Eccentricity?' *Journal of Contemporary Religion* 26:2 (2011), 225–43.

'Twenty years after the last debate on the subject in the General Synod (1987), the present study has assessed the views on Freemasonry held by senior clergy (Archdeacons, Area and Rural Deans) through a qualitative survey that attracted 518 responses (response rate: 64%).' Fascinating.

Whalen, William, *Christianity and American Freemasonry* (San Francisco: St Ignatius, 1998)

From a Roman Catholic perspective. [m02/16422 DSC]

Also in the Latimer Studies series

Thomas Cranmer. Using the Bible to Evangelize the Nation *by Peter Adam*

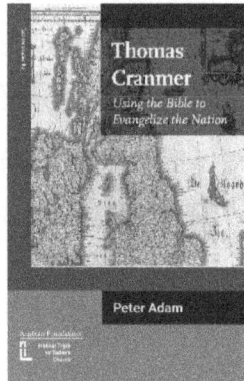

We need not only to do evangelism, but also develop contemporary gospel strategies which we trust, under God, will be effective. We need gospel wisdom, as well as gospel work. We need to work on local evangelism, but also work on God's global gospel plan. This alerts us to our own nation, as well as other nations. Gospel strategy includes the question, 'How should we evangelise our nation?' Thomas Cranmer, Archbishop of Canterbury 1532-56, strategised and worked to do this from the perspective of Anglican Reformed theology and practice. We cannot duplicate his plan in detail, but he can inspire us, and also teach us the key ingredients of such a plan.

His context of ministry had advantages and disadvantages! Our context has the same mixture. We can also learn from Cranmer's ability to work effectively in his context, despite the many problems, and the suffering he endured. God used him to evangelise his nation at his time. May God use us for his gospel glory!

Focus on Jesus: Handel's Messiah by *Robert Bashford*

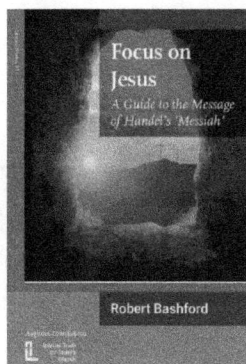

This book provides a commentary on the message of Messiah. Handel's great oratorio gives a marvellous portrayal of the Person and Work of Jesus Christ: the anticipation of his coming, his birth, his ministry, his sufferings and death, his resurrection and his ascension – plus also the proclamation of the Gospel to the world, and Christian assurance of resurrection life beyond death.

The main focus of this study is the selection of Bible verses that make up the work, compiled by the librettist Charles Jennens. At the same time there is also a certain amount of comment on the music, showing how Handel's distinctive skill contributes towards clearly expressing the message.

The aim of the book is that readers may deepen their understanding of the Bible passages included in the work and enjoy Handel's Messiah all the more – and as a result know Christ better.

Other recommendations

'Doubt not ... but Earnestly Believe' A fresh look at the BCP Baptism Service by *Mark Pickles*

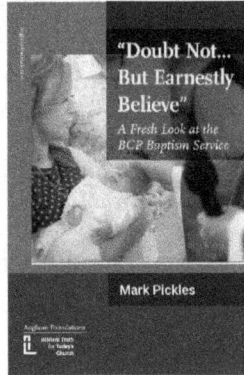

Whilst Common Worship (2000) provides a Book of Common Prayer Communion (BCP) in modern English, sadly there is no such provision for the BCP baptism service. For some Anglican evangelicals this may not seem to be a particularly regrettable omission.

There are those who might not be persuaded of the biblical mandate for baptising infants, whilst others might have concerns over some of the language used that may appear to affirm 'baptismal regeneration'. This booklet is an attempt not only to engage with those questions and concerns but also to proffer an enthusiastic support for the theology and liturgical content of the BCP Baptism service. It has a great emphasis on the covenantal grace of God which encourages Christian parents to "doubt not – but earnestly believe" in God's faithfulness and mercy. In so doing it directs our primary focus to our promise keeping God and not to ourselves.

To Tell the Truth. Basic questions and Best explanations
by *J. Andrew Kirk*

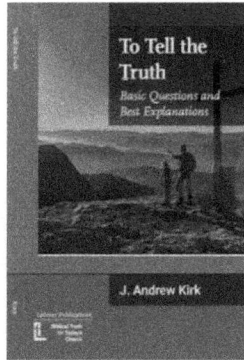

Human beings are inquisitive people. We all, quite rightly, like to explore the real world in its many fascinating dimensions. In particular, there are a few deep questions that most people face at some time in their lives: Who are we? Is there an overall purpose for our lives? What is good to believe? Why is there so much evil and suffering around? How is evil to be overcome and suffering accounted for? What best can help us to know how we should live? What is truth and how can we know it?

For well over a millennium and a half the Christian Faith has guided the Western world and, more recently, other parts of the world in how to answer these and many other questions. However, its answers have also been strongly disputed, sometimes with hostile intent. In this book, Andrew Kirk argues strongly that the Christian Faith, in spite of all that has been thrown against it, still represents by far and away the best explanations for these profound enigmas of life. Here you will find convincing answers, and reasons why alternative ideas do not ultimately match the full realities of our existence.

Living in Love and Faith. A concise Introduction and Review by *Martin Davie*

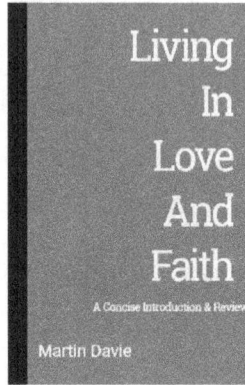

Living in Love and Faith (LLF) is set of resources produced by the bishops of the Church of England to help Christians discern God's will on the issues of 'identity, sexuality, relationships and marriage.' This booklet helps Evangelical clergy and laity approaching the LLF resources for the first time by addressing the two key questions about them. What do the LLF resources contain? What are we to make of them theologically? Everyone in the Church of England is being encouraged to engage with the LLF resources during the coming year. This booklet is an ideal place to begin that engagement.

www.ingramcontent.com/pod-product-compliance
Lightning Source LLC
Chambersburg PA
CBHW020602030426
42337CB00013B/1181

* 9 7 8 1 9 0 6 3 2 7 7 0 5 *